The 7-Figure

Side Hustle

aka

"The Million Dollar Side Hustle & Greatness"

by

Raymond Hardy

Hardy, Raymond
The 7 Figure Side Hustle
Raymond Hardy © 2017. pp. 298
Reference Listing pp
ISBN-13:978-1541195455

ISBN-10:1541195450

1. Self-Help 2. Motivation 3. Relationships 4. Sports Psychology 5. Business Marketing 6. Finance 7. How-To 8.Spiritual

_____

For information contact Raymond Hardy at
CHOSEN ONE SPORTS
P.O. BOX 821446
North Richland Hills, Texas 76182
(972)CHOSEN-1
Chosen1Sports@gmail.com
www.Chosen1Sports.com
www.BigRayInternational.com
www.MillionDollarSideHustle.com
*For Speaking Engagements or Bulk Orders
Contact: (972)CHOSEN-1

How To Use this Guide.

"You are what you repeatedly do. Excellence therefore is not an act, but a habit"-Aristotle

*Special Note: The main reason you buy this book and get a plan is because **"Money doesn't come with instructions!"** It's a tool that you can use and an element of exchange, but you need to use it wisely. Even though it's made out of trees, it doesn't grow on trees (unless you have a tree farm). You can acquire it, but if you don't know what to do with it or have a plan in hand or in place it can get misplaced into the wrong hands. You've heard the old saying "If you fail to plan, you can plan to fail". Same thing can happen with your money if you don't have a plan for it. Other people have plans for your money when you don't, because it's a magnet and it attracts all kinds! (You don't want certain people, leeches or liabilities in your circle.

"A fool & his money are soon departed".

"Wisdom is the principal thing; therefore get wisdom and with all thy getting, get understanding"-Proverbs 4:7

Learn to regulate your cash flow, so that cash flow doesn't regulate you.

**Special Notes: *Have a set of pens {Red, Black, Green; a pad, binder or spiral notebook & highlighters {Yellow, Green & Blue + a voice recorder available when you read this manuscript to take notes and achieve greater results. Take your time to absorb the knowledge that it provides and don't just race or skim through the chapters because the items that you skip could hold the solutions to your challenges. To highly impact your situation, the author suggests reading this book 7-times & no less than 3-times because the first 3-times are most important (acquired knowledge} & the next (applied knowledge} are for reinforcement & application of the knowledge obtained. Repetition & positive application of knowledge obtained are key ingredients in learning. Some things you read in this book will be repeated more than once so that it can manifest into your well being.

Below is a suggested pattern for reading & studying this book to achieve optimal results and a return on your investment of time, energy and resources.

"Study to show thyself approved unto God, a workman who needeth not to be ashamed, rightly dividing the word of truth"-2 Timothy 2:15

(Read-React & enjoy, Read & Highlight; Read-Underline & Take Notes; Read-Revaluate & Refresh; Read & Recommend; Read & Re-Purchase/Invest for members of Your Team so that everybody can be on the same page! Read & WRITE YOUR OWN BOOK so that you can leave a legacy, make a difference, impact society and position yourself for future endeavors.

COLOR GUIDE

Set of pens:

{Red(*RIGHT NOW-indicates items or areas that need immediate attention; redirection or application +serious consideration for addition to your game plan.

{Black(FUTURE-indicates important concepts & ideas that you feel are important for future growth & development,

{Green(VICTORY& FINANCE-indicates any items that can help you to Win, make money, improve your situation or put you in a positive position;

{Blue(DISCUSSION-indicates areas that may be topics of discussion and needs revisiting; new information that needs to be researched, shared with others to help their situation or discussed in a round table format.

Highlighters

{Yellow(*PAY ATTENTION/CAUTION/POLISH UP YOUR GAME -indicates areas or items where you need immediate focus, attention & improvement.

{Green(GO-indicates any items that motivates you, gets you in gear, inspires you to greatness or that can help you to accomplish the task at hand.

{Light-Blue(SPECIAL INTEREST ITEMS-indicates items or areas that have special meaning, sentimental value or align with your cause or Vision;

{Orange(ALERT-indicates items or areas that may be of "High-Concern", "Time-Sensitive", need "Discretion" or where Decisions have to be made to avoid consequences & Repercussions or where "Life-Lessons" may have been learned & that you don't repeated.

Acknowledgements

This work is dedicated to a "village of people that have helped me during my journey. Complete breakdown in Chapter 30 **The Acknowledgements Chapter: aka-"*The Treasure Chapter*"** starts on page 225.

Although there are many who have contributed to my success (to many to notate or mention) I would like to give special thanks to some who have had concentrated efforts in helping me in my ascension towards greatness, because I didn't get here by myself.

.

Table of Contents

INTRODUCTION

"The 7-Figure Side Hustle"

It's 1:36am in the morning on 5/14/2014 & I'm up brain-storming as usual and the spirit gives me a new tool to add to my already successful set of works in the "Winning is a Lifestyle" series. This one is entitled "The 7-Figure Side Hustle"(aka "The Million Dollar Side Hustle & Greatness") and it is obtainable. Now the truth of the matter is that this book is not for everybody and most people could never fathom earning nor producing 1 million dollars or more within a lifetime, much less a million within a 1-10 year span.

"Everybody wants to win, but doesn't want to do "What it takes to Win"-Big-Ray (www.48LawsOfWinning.com)

The key to receiving is Believing & Having a Plan!

Follow a Plan and not a man.

If you fall short of the goal, you can still live well off of 6-figures or a high-5 figures of additional resources. *Imagine **if you were to*** *divide all of the earth's resources up among all of the earth's inhabitants, each person would be entitled to approximately $3.5 million & 5.4 acres of land*.*

- The main question is **"Are you getting "Your Fair Share"?**
- The next question is **"Do you know someone that is getting their fair share"?**
- 3rd question: **"Do you know someone that knows someone that is getting their fair share"?**

Before you even begin to fathom a "7-Figure Side Hustle" take an inventory of all that you have; those around you including those that you associate with.

"If your 5-Closest Friends aren't worth at least $500,000 collectively, then you have a lot of work to do!"- Dr. George C. Fraser

Next, visualize yourself starting/owning a multi-faceted conglomerate from the ground floor or from "scratch" if you will? Now as you transform your mind & mindset into "Game-mode or Grind mode" as you prepare to enter into this realm of "the 7-Figure Side

Hustle" imagine that you are starting a Pro Sports Franchise (**PROS GET PAID**, *Amateurs don't!*) and that you need to create several teams within the Team. (Offense, Defense, Special-Teams, Administration, Support Staff, Marketing & Promotions, Concessions & Apparel, Personnel, Scouting, Finance, Security, Parking Lot Attendants & Valet, VIP-Services, Sales staff, so on & so forth).

Now categorize the people that you have taken inventory of and *put them into one of the 3-following categories*: **CAN HELP ME;** *CAN'T **HELP ME;*** <u>**FAN IN THE STANDS!**</u>

If they can help you tell them to come on; If they can't help you tell them to "Get-On"& go about their business or get them some business in their area of expertise; If they are a Fan in the Stands, tell them to buy a ticket, get in the stands and wait for the show to begin!

Marinate on this for a day before reading the remainder of this book because *you are going to have to do some "Soul-Searching" as well as something different in order to get different results*

and one of the first things is adjusting your atmosphere & associations to facilitate a positive mental attitude in addition to a positive cash flow environment! (The definition of insanity is "doing the same thing over & over but yet expecting different results.") **Always remember that with one good idea you can eat off of it for about 10 years! With 1-Great Idea you can eat off of it for a Lifetime! Unlock your fortune and your future with one new thought or idea!** *"You were made to be Prosper!"* Now get to Brainstorming!

"You were made to be Paid!"

–Big Ray

Chapter 1

PRIORITIES: Faith, Family, Focus & Finances/ First Things First; KEEP GOD FIRST AND YOU WILL NEVER BE LAST!

"Seek ye first the kingdom of GOD and his righteousness and all these things shall be added unto you"-Mathew 6:33

"Commit to the Lord whatever you do and He will establish Your Plans"-Proverbs 16:3

"The Blessing of the Lord brings wealth, and he adds no trouble to it"-Proverbs 10:22

"Trust in the Lord with all your heart and lean not unto your own understanding"-Proverbs 3:5

Wealth is a gift from GOD, not a product of human attainment! Divine connection is your access to success.

"But without faith, it is impossible to please him for he that cometh to GOD must believe that he is, and that he is a rewarder of them that diligently seek him." Hebrews 11:6

"You have to Believe to Receive!"-Big Ray

*YOUR RELATIONSHIP WITH GOD IS ESSENTIAL TO YOUR SUCCESS!

When you surrender to GOD, that's when you can get ready to be blessed by GOD! Ask GOD to change your mindset so that you can be able to receive. He said in his word:

"That I wish above all things that you prosper and be in good health even as your soul prospers"-3: John 1:2

To be able to accomplish anything in life, one must first be able to: Conceive, Believe And Receive that the accomplishment can happen, will happen and is destined to happen! (The CBAR concept was developed by legendary Coach & noted speaker Ray

Hardy. In the sports world, they taught us an important concept to *"Always take care of home!"* Home is where the heart is, in addition to where your Family & most precious items are.

"For where your treasure is, there will your heart be also."-Mathew 6:21

The only reason men fail is due to broken focus. You must target that of which you desire the most and pursue it relentlessly.

"A man must have a job! A job is what's necessary!"-Coach Cunningham

Chapter 2
NEXT: IMAGE

Before you go into Business, **Know the Business that you are entering into** and make sure that you are doing things in a Business Like manor in addition to making sure that your Business appears worthwhile & worth doing business with!

"The first step towards making a Million Dollars is GOD on your side and a Million Dollar Smile"-Big Ray www.MillionDollarSideHustle.com

Tighten up your "Grill" and not with the kind that the rapper Paul Wall made famous and Polish Up Your Game in all aspects: (Transportation, Occupation, Wardrobe, Appearance, Hobbies, Networks & Associations, and Print-Media/Marketing Literature & Business Cards.

Image is Everything! Perception eventually becomes reality. Everything about you should say that you are Winning before a word even comes out of your mouth. Upgrade and Invest in yourself! *"There is no greater physical investment on this earth than in oneself and your offspring."* Sometimes you have to splurge on a nice outfit or two and shoes to put your "Best foot forward!"

"It's hard to lose with a fresh pair of shoes!"- Big Ray

"It's hard to cut deals with dirt on your heels"-Darlena Hearn

You have to look like a million *{or at least look like you are capable of generating a million}* in order to attract millions. It's hard to secure million dollar contacts & contracts looking like *"Discount Danny"* with a flea-market suit/swap-meet look. You have to look the part. Everyday that you leave the house or the office, it's *"Lights, Camera, and Action"* or as we used to say in the Sports & Entertainment world, it's *"**GAME-TIME**"* or *"**SHOW-TIME!**"* Just as you are constantly evaluating scenarios, situations and surroundings, someone is always watching you. Your **Preparation and Presentation** should speak for itself and open doors that the average consumer may have challenges going through.

5-Things That You Should Always Have Control Of: A relative of mine once told me when I was younger that "No matter what level you are on or whatever your plight is in life, there are *5-things that you should always have control of:* **"Always have your hair combed, Your behind washed, Teeth Brushed, Clothes cleaned & pressed, Shoes shined!"-Theopolis Benefield**

Take an extra minute or 2 at least 3-times daily to review your appearance (*as if you were campaigning for office*) and make sure that everything is in order so that when you present your products, goods or services you can put your best foot forward. If your goal is to win the Kentucky Derby, you don't want to go in looking (or smelling) like a donkey; because that's just a behind whipping waiting to happen and you are in it to Win It!

Get with a graphic arts person and create a business card that is outstanding (not necessarily too busy or ultra flamboyant) that gives the impression that you are a winner and if put in a fish-bowl of business cards it would get selected. Also look into getting the oversized version which makes your card hard to lose when you give it to someone.

*Put Some Show-Business into your Show or Business! When trying to attract new customers, clients or patrons, you need to do something to attract a moment of someone's attention. If you see the need to use "Smoke & Mirrors", a few "props" or go "Hollywood", then by all means do so because "if your house catches on fire people will come from miles around to watch it burn down!" Do something different to make your business stand out in a crowd or better yet give the consumer something Outstanding to make sure that Your Business Stands Out In Their MIND or is a Memorable Experience!

*__*Special Note:*__ Whatever you promise in your marketing medium make sure that you fully deliver on and don't cut short! Meet, beat or exceed their expectations, because if you don't, somebody else will, which will* *make the need to utilize your services obsolete!*

**Always take the time to bless those who are a blessing to you and "treat Loyalty like Royalty" whenever possible of which we will expound upon more in a later chapter. This will go a long way towards building a positive image.

Chapter 3
AFTERWARDS: *SET A GOAL*:

"A Goal is a Dream with a Deadline"-Herm Edwards.

"I can do all things through Christ who strengthens me"-Philippians 4:13

You must become a Visionary! The bible states that *"without a vision the people shall perish"* -Proverbs 29:18

"write the vision down and make it plain on tablets so that he who reads can run with it"-Habakkuk 2:2

"Blessed is the man who finds wisdom, the man who gains understanding."-Proverbs 3:13

*"What you do for a living should be your Hobby. **What the world does for a living should be Your Business**!"*-Warren Buffet

Goal setting is the figuring out of what

your purpose, mission or that of which you are working to achieve, acquire or encompass at a point in time.

A lot of people fail to achieve or experience success because they go through life" *Misguided and undecided"*, lacking in direction if you will. Traveling in "*Circles and cycles"* sometimes causes people to become complacent and or to receive lackluster results.

Whatever profession, field of work or endeavor that you choose to encompass, you goal should focus on excelling at finding ways to perform or execute your tasks more productively and achieve greater results

Your Profit is in your Passion! You must find your "Niche"!

Figure out what your Specialty, Purpose or Mission is, or something that you like to do or that you are good at or can do well and duplicate your efforts.

Establish **what it is that you are trying to achieve?** Qualify this goal by asking yourself the following questions: "is it obtainable & maintainable" and "what does it take to make it happen"? Am I willing to do what it takes to obtain this goal and am I willing to do what it takes to maintain after achieving this goal?

Special Note: *Never make a Permanent decision based upon a temporary situation. Remember that as life evolves and you matriculate through the life-cycle, your goals and aspirations change with new experiences and relationships so be prepared to "**adapt & adjust your game to fit the terrain"** {of which we will talk about in another chapter) and update your goals continuously. Also, when you evaluate and assess your goals & aspirations, you will notice some things that you may want to discard from your program to help you to **"eliminate time-wasting".** This is one of the main reasons why you want to have goals set is so that you can have a target of which to focus your efforts, energy, resources and attention upon to accomplish the task at hand.*

Chapter 4
GET A PLAN

"Where there is no vision, the people shall perish..."-Proverbs 29:18

"Commit to the Lord whatever you do and He will establish Your Plans"-Proverbs 16:3

"A Goal without a Plan is just a wish or a dream"?-Herm Edwards

"Follow a Plan and not a man nor a woman"! "Learn how to play chess instead of checkers and once you master the art of chess flip the board over and learn how to play Backgammon & Acey-ducey"-Big Ray

"Everyone has 'the dream.' To make your dream a reality you need the plan, the process, the people, the persistence, the patience, and the passion."- Jeffrey Gitomer

*"Poor People plan for Saturday night, **Rich People plan for 3-generations.**"*

A Goal is a destination or the place where you want to be. A Plan is a

"Road-map" of how to get there; a *"Blueprint"* of how to put it together when you arrive and a *"Recipe"* of all of the ingredients, processes and tools necessary to bring it to fruition or manifest.

The Next Step after you figure out your purpose, mission or that which you are working to achieve, acquire or encompass is to develop a Plan of action or **a *"Road-map"* of how to get to the place called *"There"*.**

Game-planning or setting a Strategy is **a Blueprint for Success**! Achievers are detailed oriented. Develop a blueprint, pattern or diagram to achieve your goals. In this blueprint or pattern, *describe how you will solve problems, provide value & reward for your prospective clients (because you will receive no reward until you do so. $ is a reward you receive when you solve problems for others.)* Make sure that your motives are clear and honest and that your plan is detailed to answer the following questions: Who, what, when, where, how & why?

"If it doesn't make dollars, save money or solve problems, it doesn't make sense and if you don't have any, how much is your opinion worth?"-Big Ray

*Special Note: *The main reason you buy this book and get a plan is because **"Money doesn't come with instructions!"** It's a tool that you can use and an element of exchange, but you need to use it wisely. Even though it's made out of trees, it doesn't grow on trees (unless you have a tree farm). You can acquire it, but if you don't know what to do with it or have a plan in hand or in place it can get misplaced into the wrong hands. You've heard the old saying "If you fail to plan, you can plan to fail". Same thing can happen with your money if you don't have a plan for it. Other people have plans for your money when you don't, because it's a magnet and it attracts all kinds! (You don't want certain people, leeches or liabilities in your circle.*

"A fool & his money are soon departed".

"Wisdom is the principal thing; therefore get wisdom and with all thy getting, get understanding"-Proverbs 4:7

Learn to regulate your cash flow, so that cash flow doesn't regulate you.

***Special Note:** Design your game plan so that it's rewarding for those on your team to be in your presence in addition to those who subscribe to your products, goods and services.*

****Special Note:** For those of you whose goal is to accumulate a million dollars within a year's time, your plan should encompass making at least $2,739 a day {or more for 365-days straight. This goal which may be or seem unfathomable to an average consumer shouldn't be hard to accomplish if you have the right mindset, product, services, enthusiasm & the right people on your team.*

Chapter 5
GET UP OFF OF YOUR BEHIND &
DO SOMETHING ABOUT IT!

"All Hard Work Leads to Profit, but mere talk only leads to Poverty."-Proverbs 14:23

"You will always remain the same until the pain of remaining the same becomes too great".

"If you don't Prospect, you don't prosper".

"You are what you repeatedly do. Excellence therefore is not an act, but a habit"-Aristotle

A lot of people over analyze the plan and fail to act on the idea itself. Utilize the "KISS" method {which stands for Keep It Short & Simple} and put some action behind the idea. Most of the time, a plan will encompass *"Goals & objectives"*, Responsibilities & Resources necessary to complete & maintain the project + answer the following Questions: *Who; What; When; Where, Why & How? The main reason many Great Ideas never get off of the ground is that a lot of people talk too much and fail to act, react or* **follow up** *to make sure that the idea comes to fruition.* The Bible tells you that

"All Hard Work Leads to Profit, but mere talk leads only to Poverty"-Proverbs 14:23

The only thing standing in the way of YOUR SUCCESS is Atmosphere & Your Fear! Create or Find a **SYSTEM** (*Save Yourself Time, Energy, Money*), Product or Service and Duplicate Your Efforts! "Prior Preparation Prevents Poor Performance: If your destination is Greatness, then prepare for your destiny! (Google Search: "Greatness is not a Coincidence"!) Do not wait for Greatness to arrive to prepare because your lack of preparation or procrastination could result in less than great results. Prepare for Greatness and your efforts & preparation will attract Greatness! **The biggest proponent to success is "FEAR"\ False Evidence Appearing Real.** I remember a few times in my sports career as a Coach that we as a staff on a couple of teams went into a few games believing that we were going to get our hat handed to us because of lack of this or they had that or differences in development of personnel. As a player I never had this problem because I was always taught to **be a difference maker, to always play to win & to Hit Hard and Never Quit!** Instilled in me were certain principles, values & mottos that I still utilize in my philosophy today such as **"A Winner is not a quitter and a quitter is not a Winner"; "You'll Win if You Don't Quit",**

"There's no "I" in TEAM, but there is 1 in Champion & 1 in WIN + 2 in CHAMPIONSHIP"!

We were taught to believe in what we were doing and to visualize being successful/achieving our goals. We were taught **to always have a Positive Mental Attitude** & that if we didn't believe that we could win to not show up for the game or event! *"Losing" was not in our vocabulary!* If you can't help the team, don't hurt the TEAM! It is better to have a few with earnest efforts than to have many with lukewarm enthusiasm!

Now that you have your mind right or in the right frame of mind **to be $uccessful, YOU HAVE TO PUT IN SOME WORK!**

"All Hard Work leads to Profit, Mere talk only leads to Poverty"-Proverbs 14:23

The only place in life where "*Success*" comes before "*Work*" is in the dictionary (and Webster still had to work before his dictionary became successful)! **You must have a "Willingness" to do what is required!** In order to transform your Goals into $uccess, you have to be willing to work hard, consistently and continually to improve your situation to be the Best "You" that you can be!

*You Beat 50% of the competition just by Working Hard!

*You Beat 40% more just by doing what's Right!

*The Last 10% is a Dog-fight!

It's not the size of the dog in the fight, but more so the size of the Fight in the Dog. You have to condition your mind to operate in "$uccess-Mode" instead of "Stress-mode". Most people due to their limited perspective, background or dispensation cannot fathom nor see past barriers, boxes, obstacles or walls and break down at the first sight of adversity even though they may be fully equipped to handle the situation at hand. You on the other hand are more than a conqueror and you have to learn how to awaken and unleash that CHAMPION that is inside of YOU! When faced with an obstacle or adversity you will find a way to Win, overcome obstacles and think "Outside of the Box."

Currently you are sitting on top of a "Gold-Mine!" The only problem is that the gold is not going to get up and mine itself & hop into your pocket. If you want it, you are going to have to dig & work to get it. It's there if you want it, but are you going to do what it takes to get it out? *The only place where Success comes before Work is in the Dictionary (and Webster had to work to get that in there).*

"HARD-WORK PAYS OFF!"-Devin Wyman

__Special Note:__ Before beginning this process of adjusting your attitude, thought processes & belief system, ask yourself these questions to eliminate "Time-wasting": #1) How bad do you want "It" or need "It"? #2) Are you willing to do what it takes to obtain "It"? #3) Are you willing to do what it takes to maintain 'It" once "It" is obtained? Next, there are 2-types of people: "Can-Do" & "Won't-Do", which one is You?

Chapter 6
KEEP THINGS IN PROPER PERSPECTIVE: MAKE THE $ & DON'T LET THE $ MAKE YOU!

You Must Have Balance in Your Life!

"The 2-most important days in your life are the day that you are born & the day you find out why"-Steve Harvey.

"Every day after you brush your teeth in the morning, look in the mirror and repeat after me 3-times {with enthusiasm: **I was made to be PAID!***"-Big Ray*

Keep discovering "*Why*". **Understand that you always must be in control of your destiny and not let destiny control you.** Never jump for $ or appear desperate. *Never let a prospect or project manipulate or pressure you into any situation*. No matter how much money you are offered, never let anyone use money to control you. *Money is a tool and an inanimate object. It is supposed to serve and work for you* *instead of you serving and working for it*. You are supposed to give $ assignments and tasks to complete. Money is a resource and a reward for solving problems for others, not a source. Know where your true source is and where your blessings & power come from.

No man can serve both GOD and mammon.

"...Choose you this day whom you shall serve, as for me and my house, We Will Serve The Lord!" –Joshua 24:15

The way you make money is by solving problems for others. The best way to do this is to find your *"niche"*; a specialized skill; problems that need to be solved or needs, wants & desires that need to be fulfilled. **Be the Best at whatever it is that you are doing!** If you are currently in an occupation that's not particularly to your liking or where you would like to be, then do the best you can where you're at until you can get to where you want to be. Remember, someone is always watching you and you never know who might be the next one to come up and take you with them just because of your work ethic or approach to life?

For those of you starting off from a lower-economic status, don't look at other people's "perceived" success or get caught up in the material items until you can afford them (or can't afford not to have them) nor get led astray or down the wrong road to acquire status symbols or "fast-lane" money. The same effort that someone utilizes to gain things by nefarious means or sell dope can be used to sell soap or provide other products & services that are essential to life and receive the same profit margin without the excessive risk factors. All you have to do is to think outside of the box & use your head for something other than a "hat-rack!" A prime example of this is the countless amounts of students that we mentor before they go to college and as they matriculate past graduation. We explain to them that the main reason people go to college is to learn how to make money. The only thing that they don't tell you in college is that you don't have to wait until you graduate to start making money *contrary to popular belief.*

We explain to them that Success in Life is a Team Effort as well as a *"Number's Game"* and that you will need a certain number of people to subscribe to your theories, products or services to get ahead. This is why we suggest that they attend a College or University with an at least 5k-10k minimum amount of enrolled students in an area that has access to a major airport and a bus or train station because currency travels and circulates. Of all of the people you will meet, 85-92% of them will use some type of cleansing product/products to bathe, clean or wash their body; hair; clothes; dishes; bathroom, autos and appliances. In addition, 65-85% will utilize some type of personal products {Toothpaste, deodorant, mouth-wash, skin-care product, hygiene items, cologne or perfumes, etc) hair preparation products {shampoo, conditioner, pomade, lotions, gels, tonics, hair-sprays & more.) Approximately 35-40% or more of the students will utilize outside sources {not supplied by the school) of Electronic items, Electricity, Internet, Cable, Cell-Phone service, Laundry or Dry Cleaning services, Transportation, Auto-maintenance/Repair, articles of clothing, shoes & athletic wear, Food. I could go on & on, but hopefully you get the picture. 2-Words, *"Supply & Demand!"* If you could service just a mere 3-6% of the population on a consistent basis such as once or twice a month at a minimum profit margin of $5-20 off of each in that percentage you will then discover why the "*College days*" will be some of the best days of your life. *Imagine sponsoring a social event in college twice a month & attracting 150-300 patrons at a cost of $10 per head admission pre-purchase/$15-20 at the door, with an approximate overhead of $200-400? Now imagine if you found 9-10 other college students with earnest enthusiasm who were a little short on their cash/or wanted extracurricular income or complementary entertainment and offered them free admission, food/beverages during event & $20-40+ (at the end of event in addition to breakfast, lunch or dinner at the IHOP, Denney's, Waffle-House, the local Buffet or any other (late-night) eatery of your choice) to help you to market, promote & facilitate operation of the event?*

Now that you are *"Grown-Man or Woman"* status, imagine if you figured out a way to provide essential services (those services that are essential to life that people were going to utilize on a regular basis such as Electricity, Cell-Phone, Internet, Cable, Insurance, Coffee/Tea, Vitamin/Health-food products, Transportation or otherwise that they were going to utilize with or without you) and offered them to family, friends & neighbors at a discounted or broker's rate which would be less than what they were paying? Now, just like the *"College Student"* imagine if you found 9-10 people with earnest enthusiasm who were short on their cash/ or wanted extracurricular income and offered them free admission/tickets to social events, food/beverages during events & at eateries around town + an opportunity to make approximately $200-4000+ in additional income a month to help you to market, promote & facilitate the recruiting of people to subscribe to these goods & services? Now throw in the option to acquire fresh luxury autos and trips abroad at discounted rates or possibly sponsored when certain levels of productivity are obtained &

maintained over a consistent period of time and see how much the enthusiasm and demand for your product and services increases?

Remember, people usually spend their money in 7-main areas: Church, Food, Hair, Clothing, Automobiles; Entertainment & Housing. Get your hand in at least 3 or more of the aforementioned and keep connections in all 7 and you can prosper significantly.

Special Note: You don't have to have the lowest price in town, just be consistent, competitive, and different/unique & respected. People will pay for convenience and quality & buy the heck out of different & unique.

"Everybody you meet can do at least 2 things for you, it's up to you to determine what those 2 things are" –Penney St. James

Chapter 7
GET THE RIGHT PLAYERS, COACHES & MENTORS ON YOUR TEAM: ALIGN YOURSELF WITH POSITIVE/PRODUCTIVE PEOPLE:

"Success in Life is a Team-Effort"!-Big-Ray.

"Team-Work makes the Dream Work!"-Marshal Fortson

The acronym "T.E.A.M" stands for (Together Everybody Achieves More!

"If you want to be Great, surround yourself with Greatness! If you want to be Rich, surround yourself with Riches or Rich People. You usually get what you get around!" -Big-Ray

"If you wear a 3-piece suit & nice shoes and work in a barn all day, you will come home smelling like horses & hay!"-Big Ray.

"People make the wrong choices listening to the wrong voices!"-Devin Wyman

*With good help being hard to find, always stay in *"Recruit"* mode to keep quality-effective people on your team. If you're not networking, you're not working!

"Sometimes you don't have to be a Rocket Scientist; sometimes you just need a Rocket!"-Big Ray

Develop a visual depth chart of all of the different positions you will need assembled on your Team. (i.e.; Accountant, Bookkeeper, Financial-Advisor

*make sure that these 3-positions are held by 3 different individuals that are not associated with one another so that you can create a checks & balances system. *Also, Never take financial advice from someone whose income is based on the information that they give you.*

Attorney {2-3, Marketing Team, Promoters, Webmaster {2-3, Graphic Artists {3-5, Medical Doctor,

*Hype-Man {2-3 minimum}. *This is a very important position on your team! You never know how much you need this person until things get tight or you get behind in the game! You will need one for the fans or in the crowd to rally people around your cause and another one for the team, sales-force or workers! (Depending on how big your business/company or entity becomes you will need the 3rd one for yourself when the other 2 are occupied.* **Leaders need Love, Inspiration, and Motivation & Encouragement too!** *Remember, the game (whatever line of business that you are in) is 90% mental.* **As a Leader, you need to keep your "creative juices" flowing so that you can keep the business going!** *Not only do you need to be motivated & inspired to lead, you need a motivated & inspired team, sales-staff, congregation or workers, in addition to the need for motivated & inspired potential prospects & new clientele. Nothing beats a motivated potential prospect that has the willingness* *and ability to purchase (except a paying customer/loyal client.) Ideal candidates for this position are: A Pastor/Evangelist, A Coach, A former Athlete or Cheerleader; Used-car Salesmen; Someone who has been successful at Sales/Multi-Level Marketing with good closing techniques; A Radio show host, A popular DJ or someone that has a high level of energy with a lot of enthusiasm that is contagious. The person in this position should have a unique personality, be a great communicator and have a specialized set of skills in that they can graphically illustrate a vision, theme or **IDEA** in a short amount of time (to arouse **Interest**) and have it manifesting within a matter of minutes(to create a **Desire.**) Classic illustrations of this concept are: "Someone who could sell water to a whale or ice & igloo's to an Eskimo". In essence you need someone that can preach a good sermon, get the crowd up out of their seat, on their feet to cheer (**Energy/**a change of momentum) & put their hands together clapping to give you, your team or cause a standing ovation! (**Action** or motion in the direction of your goal or game-plan.)*

*Chiropractor {2-3. *Get your spine aligned on a regular basis. It's hard for you to perform at your highest capacity if your body is tight, in pain or not feeling good or Great! Most problems with the body are due to sub-lactations or misalignment of the spine. You want the mind to control the body & not the body controlling the mind. The body is controlled by the brain sending messages through the central nervous system. If the spine is misaligned or a nerve pinched, it could cause certain parts of the body to miss or not receive all of the signals that the brain is sending at the time the signals are sent.*

Barber & Hair-Stylist {2-3. *Never discount the value of a Great Barber or Hair-Stylist. Not only is "the quickest way to come up a fresh cut" (or style) as far as image consciousness & self-esteem goes. Now-a-days, your hair-care technician is more than someone that does your hair & keeps you looking good in front of your potential customers & clients. They are an integral part of your business whether you realize it or not? A lot of them have been to college or* *universities other than Barber & Beauty College. A large portion of them are entrepreneurs & CEO's of their own companies. To stay in business they have had to develop negotiation, conflict resolution, marketing, recruitment & communication skills in addition to being able to deal with complex & varied personalities to achieve satisfaction & optimal results. They have to be: an image consultant, fashion expert, a procurement specialist; a confidant, a Spiritual guide; a love-Doctor, cheer-leader, alternative funding source: financial advisor, actor/entertainer (hair-shows, marriage counselor, social event guide, Business Referral Partner in addition to being an overall "Solution Specialist". The more diversified their clientele base is, the more valuable they can be to your team. All you have to do is tap into the source and ask questions (& ask for referrals). Chances are that whatever you are looking for to aide you in your business they have connections to and can possibly get you a discounted rate. Not only that, most Successful Barbers & Stylists wants to see you Successful because it would make their business more attractive by having you as a client and mutually beneficial in that it further enhances your ability to subscribe to their services & refer/attract new clients as well. A lot of times back when I was in the hair industry in the off-seasons, I actually made more money from the connections I made in the salon than I made from managing & being a barber-stylist in one. Not only do people from all socio-economic conditions come through Beauty & Barber salons all across America, for those of you caught up in your work, it keeps you in touch with current events & trends.*

Maid & Janitorial Services {2-3: They taught us when I was in the Restaurant business that the most important people in the building were the janitor & pot-washer.

Personal Trainers {2, Personal Bodyguards/Security on call {3 or more, Personal Drivers/Chauffeur's {2-3, Limo Services on call {2-5, Gym Memberships {1-2,

Executive Secretary {1-2 and note, this person needs to be someone that is extremely trustworthy, professional and

someone that you don't have an intimate relationship with,

Dentist, Real-Estate Agent{2-3, Auto-Brokers{3+, Travel agents{2-3, Airline Employees{3+, Hotel Employees{3+, Millionaires {no less than 6, but the more the merrier, Ghost-Writers{2-3, Publicist{2-3, Club Owners {3-5, Restaurant Owners {10+, Professional Athletes {@ least 3 or more in each sport especially Football, Basketball, Baseball, Boxing, Wrestling, Hockey, Moving Company{2-3,

*Handyman/ Equipment Manager {2-3(_Believe it or not, this guy is going to be one of the most important people on your team._ *Most people won't appreciate this person until something goes wrong of at which time you are going to need a "Solution Specialist". The more versatile the person that holds this position is, the better off you are going to be (i.e., Paint, clean up, hang drywall/sheet-rock, move furniture, plumbing skills, stand in for security, minor electrical skills, computer repairs skills & more.) This person needs to be someone that possess high integrity, extremely trustworthy,* *professional and someone you can trust with keys to your business to take care of after-hours issues and not give the store/business away nor sell trade secrets to the competition. {Excellent candidates for this position would be middle-aged males with stable backgrounds that are family/team oriented like a pastor or little league coach that needs to make some extra $ on the side.*

Attractive Hosts for Special Events {10+ Female & 5-Male, Barbershop & Salon Owners {10-20, Personal Assistants-PA's {2-3,

Network Marketers{5+/ie;Amway, Primerica, 5-Linx, Avon, Mary Kay, Social Media Zing, Visalis, Kyani, Noni, Pre-Paid Legal, Excel, Herbalife, Stream, Advocare}; *Just like the "Hype-Man" the Network Marketer comes in real handy. A lot of people knock them or avoid them like the "plague" because a lot of people have been conditioned to stay in their disposition & don't want to hear the truth about Corporate America "brain-washing them", being "Modernized-Slavery" or "Trading time for $". I embrace them. A lot of them offer a plan* for obtaining wealth in addition to quality products/ services that enhance the quality of life or save you money over a period of time. On the business side, the one's that have been in business a long time have developed proven $uccess-Systems that if you tap into them you can share some of that $uccess as well! A lot of times as a business owner in the guise of expanding or improving your business you will search out new concepts, ideas or people that you can plug into your business to help it flourish; Besides, a lot of times they have done a lot of the ground work for you and saved you the up front $. All you have to do is **observe, take notes & learn!** (They usually provide a nice venue/place in which to have the events/meetings; They have target-marketed, invited & provided a large group of pre-screened, motivated & enthusiastic business minded people who are open to making extra-$ outside of what they do or need a job. **A lot of the people that you will meet at these events will be opinion leaders and people with substantial contacts or a warm-market if you will {This is what they refer to as "Impact-**

Players", "Game-Changers" or an individual with the ability to change the game and your bank account as a single entity). Next, if the meeting is over 2-3 hours, they sometimes provide a nice lunch/refreshments & samples of their products/services. In addition, they usually fly in a Motivational Speaker, Guest-Speaker or **"Hype-Man"** that will deliver a Sermon/**"Hype-Speech"** so compelling & inspiring that has you feeling so great at the end that you will feel like you just won the Super-bowl & want to lay your hard earned $ down at the podium and sign up now! Next they provide advanced training classes and marketing techniques that you could easily adapt and utilize within your own business to help it to grow and prosper. Now if you notice, a lot of these informational meetings also known as "Introduction & Attraction" Sessions will be strategically choreographed/orchestrated as to where they have timed "restroom & water-breaks" where you will meet people you don't know {some who are in the business who want to gauge your level of interest in the business & others who aren't) who want to get your opinion as to what you think about the presentation? This is your opening to Network, ask questions & inquire of the person's background and dispensation. Collect and exchange as many business cards, cell #'s & email addresses as possible during these breaks because at the end of these meeting a lot of the non-enrolled people will cordoned off or pulled over to the side as the person who invited them & their up-line try to persuade, motivate and inspire or "close" non-enrollee's to sign up ASAP with a "sense of urgency" or a "divide & conquer move".)

All you have to do is go and visit a few of their major meetings or conventions and network to come up. The good thing about most of these meetings is that **they have prescreened most of the invitees to include people that are "open minded", have their options open for new concepts and idea, plus are "like minded/business minded individuals".** Everything or everyone you need to build a team usually shows up at these meetings from owners, customers & clients to worker bees. Everybody plays an important part in the ecosystem

"Everybody you meet can do at least 2-things for you! It's up to you to find out what those 2-things are & fully utilize them to that extent."-Penney St. James

+*Special Note:* *Don't take this as a sign to join every Multi-level company that comes along, because they aren't for everybody. You don't have to join to benefit from them or their products & services. Besides, you can develop your own Multi-level company just like they did, it just takes effort. Also if they have product or services that can improve your life, are ecologically friendly and/or save you time, energy & resources its alright to spend a little $ with them on products/services that you were going to acquire anyway. When it comes down to it, people like to spend $ with those that they know or like. In the grand scheme of things, you were going to wash your body, hair, clothes & dishes in addition to use electricity, internet, insurance, cable & cell phone services with or without them. It wouldn't hurt to patronize their business if they are going to patronize yours. (You may even run across a Multi-level company that you like and can see yourself profiting from?)*

Remember, everybody has to eat and it's enough out here for everybody to have a smorgasbord or a Buffet! The word for today is "Mutually-Beneficial"! What is it to spend a couple of hundred dollars on some soap-products or otherwise with someone who will turn around and spend Thousands with you?

Party Promoters {5-10; These are usually people who have large followings & databases. As you mature, get older or more prominent in your business you will have less time or desire to hit every "happy-hour", party or new night-club that comes along. For less than a few hundred dollars on the average you can cross-promote/ tap into their databases or onto their print mediums and present your marketing message to the multitudes for less time, energy & effort than it would have taken you to do it yourself. Most promoters won't mind assisting you because not only will they have a new client, but they can take your small seed & multiply it up to times ten making this venture "Mutually Beneficial".

__Special Note:__ Before approaching a promoter about cross-promoting make sure that your product, service or marketing message doesn't cause a conflict of interest nor conflict with your standards, morals, values, ethics or religious beliefs? Sometimes it's better to pay extra up front and get a direct promoter or marketing medium to advertise your goods & services in a positive manner, than to portray an image contradictory to that intended just to save a dime or a dollar somewhere and distort your brand or image.

Uniform manufacturers {3+, Energy Drink manufacturers {2-3, Sports Drink Suppliers {2-3, Sports Shoe Representatives {3+, Screen Printers {3+, Comedians {7+, Professional Singers {7+, Parking Valet companies {2-3, Chefs{3+, Catering companies {3+, BBQ-Cooks{3-5, Event Planners {3, Book Authors{5+, Skin-Care Manufacturers{3+, Pastors{7+, Concert Promoters {5+, Play Writers {3+, DJ's {4+, Electrician{2, Plumber{2, Computer Technician{2-3,

Special Note: If you can find a person or individuals that can do 3+ or more of the above as a single entity and still be highly effective, you have found what we like to call an "Impact-Player", Franchise-Player, "Game-Changer", Superstar or Super-Hero! _These are people who can play multiple positions and still achieve optimal Results! If you are going to develop a **CHAMPIONSHIP TEAM it pays to have some **Team Players with Superstar Qualities!** (You don't want too many Superstars, just Team members with Superstar qualities to achieve balance & equilibrium. You do not want egos & attitudes getting in the way of progress or Success!). Remember that everybody on the Team plays an important part. Later on in this book (The Acknowledgements Chapter) I will introduce you to some of the people on my team that have helped me to become $uccessful and if you need assistance mention that you heard about them from the author or by reading this book and turn some of your challenges into $olutions! {If you talk to them nice & ask for the "Big-Ray $pecial" you'll be surprised at what you might get! They may_ be able to help you to find some $olutions to your challenges at a reduced rate.

*** **_Special Note:_** Do not forget to reward, recognize or give a "Love-offering" periodically to your team-members or associates when you are Victorious or for a job well done. Also, if things ever get tight, these are the people that you will reach out to call on for favors. Remember Rich people call in favors, Poor people don't!

****<u>**_Special Note:_**</u> **Team up with people that accessorize your limitations, accentuate your weaknesses & are enemies of your weaknesses. Also, make sure that their philosophy harmonizes with your objectives.**

Chapter 8
$UPER HERO STATUS

You can develop a 7-Figure Side Hustle aka "Greatness" much faster once you acquire or achieve *"Super-Hero Status." In order to achieve Super Hero Status you must possess at least 3 or more of the following: A website, A Little League Team or Youth Organization, A Book that you have authored, a Radio Show, A Clothing Line, A Barbershop/Salon, A Car Wash, Church, Restaurant/Sports-Bar, Car Dealership, Apartment Complex/Rental Properties, A Professional and/ or Minor-League Team or Organization; A Hit Record, A Theme Song, a Signature Product Line or Service that you have developed {that can be verified.*

When you were younger, a "Super-Hero" was someone who could come along out of nowhere and save the day. Now-a-days, a $uper-hero is not only someone who can come along and save your day, but also someone who can help you to get ahead, increase and/or help you to save your Business, Home or Auto; A "Difference-Maker", "Game-Changer" or an "Impact-

Player" if you will. Start making a difference in someone's life today. Something small in your eyes could amount to something huge in someone else's world. Don't be afraid to, nor forget to give back to and plant seeds of "Greatness" into the community, Churches & civic organizations as you ascend the ladder of "Greatness!" This helps to build a good name, relationships & rapport within the community in addition to a future harvest.

Special Note:

 With $uccess in Life being a Team-Effort, you are going to need as many avenues as you can get to promote your product, service, theme or cause in the guise of Branding/Marketing and Name Recognition. It's a numbers game. In order to achieve your goal, you will need a certain number/quantity and quality of people to subscribe to your theory, products or services.

**Special Note*: Once you reach Super-Hero status, you will find it most beneficial to acquire a "side-kick", confidant, protégée, mentor, wise-counselor, pastor, consultant, Uncle/Aunt, barber/hair-stylist or someone* *that you can discuss your dreams, goals & aspirations with in addition to the challenges that you may face that will give you good sound feedback yet keep your information confidential. This should be a person of Character, Integrity & Principles that while they respect what you do, they are not caught up in all "the-hype" of what you do and will give you an honest and realistic point of view or the truth as they see it regardless of whether or not you're donating to or financing their functions or factions. This person will help to keep you rooted & grounded in your core beliefs and will more than likely bring it to your attention if they see you getting off track or headed in the wrong direction. Being "Super-Hero" status isn't an easy job, (even though a lot of us make it seem easy or effortless because we're blessed by GOD to be talented & gifted to perform or produce well in our areas of expertise. Sometimes it's lonely at the top like the May-Tag repairman and other times the pressure builds up and we need somewhere to release in a positive manner without distorting our brand or image.*

Chapter 9
EFFORT, ENERGY & ENTHUSIASM:

"Everybody wants to win, but doesn't want to "Do what it takes to Win!"-Big Ray.

"If you want to be Great, You must do something Extra"-Percy Duhe.

"Always keep a Positive Mental Attitude"-Earnest Thomas

Attitude determines Altitude, Latitude & Longitude! If you do what everybody else is doing, you will get everybody else's results. If you want different results, you must do something different. One of the definitions of Insanity is doing the same thing over and over but yet expecting a different result.

"Faith without works is dead".

The 7-Figure Side Hustle is not meant to be an *"overnight sensation".* It's a Process. It is about concepts and ideas including short-term, mid-range & long-term goal setting that make sense and will help you to make sensible choices using the resources & connections that you have in order to get the results that you want. As with any proven Success System, it will work if you work it. Don't think that because you bought this book and it looks pretty on your bookshelf that some magical fairy is going to come and put a million dollars under your pillow. You have to read the book (over & over) then apply the concepts and ideas to produce a positive cash flow of extracurricular income there by creating alternative sources of income that can provide additional options as well as opportunities for you and your family. One thing about opportunities not taken advantage of, they don't just go away, they go to someone else. You want to put yourself into a position of always being able and ready to give as well as to receive.

"Energy Sells!"-Devin Wyman

Have you ever wondered why some Professional Athletes get mega-endorsement deals & commercials while the rest operate at status quo? Have you ever noticed that some of them at the end of their sports careers go on to color commentate, do Television commercials or become spokesmen for various products and services while others fade off into the regular workplace? Did you ever notice that some corporate companies when advertising to fill certain positions {especially in sales, marketing or customer service} infer that they are looking for individuals with *"High-energy"* & able to work within a team setting or atmosphere? Part of the reason for some of these scenarios is the energy that these people exude or give off. Energy sells, it's attractive, it's contagious and it's the fuel for enthusiasm. In order to attract a crowd or draw a following you must have energy {which is equivalent to action}. Have you ever noticed that when some players are selected for Mid-Season or Post-Season All-star games that some are selected for productivity while others are nominated for energy, popularity and their ability to please or entertain the crowd? Prime example: You may have a Basketball player in one market that comes to work night in & night out does his job and averages 16+points per game by playing good defense, doing basic lay-ups &

free-throws {say possibly a lay-up & 2-free-throws per quarter} and goes virtually unknown. You can have another player that averages the same 16+ points per game by doing acrobatic lay-ups, high-flying dunks and raining 3-point jumpers out of the sky or at the buzzer. Now on paper and in the final results, 16 points is equal to or equivalent to 16 points and the final scores do not tabulate nor take into account and/ or give credit for *"flair, flavor* or *"style-points"* for creativity, but the fan voting for All-star events does. Moral of the story; in order for you or your business to get elected to *"All-star-status"* by customers, clients & consumers or attract new business, you need to have the energy, flair & flavor that they savor in addition to consistently delivering great service.

Enthusiasm

"Always do the Best you can where you're at until you can get to where you want to be."-Octus Polk

"Enthusiasm Breeds Excitement!"-Mike Murdock

Always keep a positive mental attitude and have enthusiasm with everything you do. Remember, somebody is always watching you and you're constantly under surveillance. Sometimes when people are approached with a proposal, opportunity or business proposition they will sometimes step back over a period of time to observe as to how you operate independently of their assistance or association to evaluate whether or not they would like to pursue a partnership with you. In the sports realm and sometimes in business, they send out scouts or monitors to observe you in a *"natural state"* to help determine if you would have synergy and be a good fit. *(People always act differently when they think you are watching them & they do this as part of a "Checks & Balance" System to make sure that everything that comes & goes out of their door is double-checked for consistency, quality & clarity. This helps to eliminate problems & reduce challenges before they occur.)*

<u>Special Note:</u> *"Some people do what they want to do and others do what they have to* *do. This is the difference between "Stressful & Successful."-Big Ray*

With the game of Life being 90% mental, always approach it with a positive mental attitude and a mindset to dominate, not just participate. When faced with challenging situations, come with the mindset, appearance & approach of a Successful Victory!

Chapter 10
RELATIONSHIPS:
"Are you Qualified to be $atisfied?"-Big-Ray

"Never confuse Relationships with Situation-ships"-Pastor Freddie Haynes.

"Everybody you meet can do at least 2-things for you? It is up to you to determine what those 2-things are?"-Penny St. James.

"A lot of people want to win, but don't want to do what it takes to WIN!"-Big-Ray

"If your Presence can't add Value to my Life, Your Absence will make no difference!"-Big Ray

Relationships are a process of exchange. The key word for the day is *"Mutually Beneficial"*, which means that all parties involved should benefit from the Relationship{not necessarily equally because sometimes others will have more to invest or lose depending on the level of investment. There are 3-parts to a Relationship: The Physical, Financial & Communication. Of these 3, Communication is the most important because the first 2 can leave you at any moment. In any good relationship there must be good D.I.C. (Dollars, Information & Contacts. You must determine which of these that you are bringing to the table & which of these that you need? If you possess none of these, you need to reassess your vision then go and align yourself with some people that can help you to achieve/acquire your goal. Sometimes in life when you are lacking in Resources/ D.I.C. (Dollars, Information & Contacts it may be necessary to team with others for a few seasons to help them achieve their goals/aspirations to learn the system and/ or become acclimated with others who can fuel-inject your project. The acronym ***TEAM stands for: Together Everybody Achieves More***. Now a-days, you hear the buzz-word **"Team-Player"** being utilized a lot. Do not be dismayed by this term. *In corporate America we were taught that being a "Team-Player" comes about after one completes their own responsibilities to themselves.* "To thine own self be true, and then you can be true to your friends". In this quest of excellence, you must have: Character,

Integrity and Principles especially in terms of Relationships.

The "5-C's of Relationships. When gathering data to determine if you are going to move forward into a new relationship, always check for the "5-C's" which are: **Christ, Car, Crib, Credit and Career.**

Take inventory of how a potential new prospect grades out in each area and tabulate their score.

(Scoring System: Just as in the educational system you were graded out on test scores & aptitude to see if you would be promoted to the next grade level, you should grade out applicants in the relationship department to see if you want to promote them to the next level. Scoring Ratings: **C-70-79 %(Just a Friend/Associate; B-80-89 % (Potential Business Liaison/Dating Prospect; A-90%+= Potential Business Partner/Mate or Spouse.** (*Anything or anyone that scores below "C" level needs to go back for remedial studies and polish up their game a bit before trying out for your team/organization.* Remember, it takes more to be a Champion! If you don't set

"*Standards*" or have "*Criteria*" for membership on your team, you will be in for the biggest disappointment since you found out that there was "*No Santa Claus*". Use *discernment* and don't feel obligated nor obliged to entertain every "*Joe-Blow*" or "*Sally-Sue*" that comes along. Sometimes you can see *foolishness* coming from a mile away and its best to nod your head and let it pass on by.

"Be careful of whom you choose to date... A lot of people aren't looking for LOVE, they're looking for HELP."-Comedian Anastasia The Bold

"Before You Come out of Your Pocket with "Change", You better come out of your mouth with "Game" {as in "Game-Test" to make sure that it's the "Best"! - Big Ray

The "*3-B's of Relationships:* Other attributes to take into account when contemplating on entering into potential new relationships are: **Brains, Bank & Business Sense.** Pre-screening applicants for these attributes will help to alleviate many future headaches, heartaches and strife in addition to reducing tension and anxieties.

Never Defecate and Eat in the same Place! Refrain from developing or engaging in interpersonal relationships within the workplace (unless it's a family business or mutually agreed to in advance to make it official by both parties involved). Reason being is that not only can this cause both parties that are involved to lose focus & productivity but it also can negatively affect the focus & productivity of associates, co-workers and constituents as well. Not only that, but when the time comes to dissolve such relationships, they usually cause division, tension, stress and strife in the work place and could result in you seeking employment opportunities or employees elsewhere.

Pre-Screening for Future Potential:

"Are you Qualified to be Satisfied?"-Big Ray

"When you first meet someone, check out their hair, feet, hands/nails & teeth. If they

can't take care of them, they can't take care of you!"-Angie Hamlin

Just as we mentioned in an earlier chapter as to how image was important, you also need to consider the images & reputations of those that you align yourself with to make sure that it's a right fit. Just because a person or an entity is extremely attractive, talented, gifted or financially secure in a particular area doesn't necessarily mean that they are a good fit for you. In the bible it refers to passages about being equally/un-equally yoked, using wisdom & the value of a good name. In business and personal relationships you have to do a background check and check their resume/references before getting into business/bed with a new individual or entities. One mistake in this area can be the cause of major setbacks & headaches of which could cost more to get out of than the originally anticipated outcome or payoff. ***Avoid Intimate & Business Relationships with those who do not respect you, your time, and your dime or see your vision!***

When contemplating entering into new interpersonal relationships have a pad with at least 25+ or more qualities listed that you are looking for in a mate then grade out/pre-screen new applicants on a percentage basis of how they stack up against your list to eliminate wasting your time, their time or your dime! (If you didn't have at least 20-25 preferred qualities listed, you didn't give it much considerable thought & go back and think thoroughly. They should grade out at) 70% or more to be your friend; 80% or more to be a girlfriend/boyfriend & 90% or better for marriage material.) **Nobody is perfect, but there is someone perfect for you!** *This eliminates having to go through 9 or 10 candidates just to find out number 3 was the right one!*

The wrong people who are in your life don't always leave voluntarily. Sometimes you have to cut the strings & sever the ties! Other times you have to "Punt" or give them the proverbial boot to get out of a hole or a rut, reposition and get better field position. Self-preservation is essential! GOD sends people into our lives for a Reason, a Season or a Lifetime! It is up to us to discern what their purpose is in our lives and fully utilize it to that extent. Everybody you meet can do at least 2-things for you? It is up to you to determine what those 2-things are.

Special Note: **Before beginning this process of Pursuing new Relationships, ask yourself these questions to eliminate "Time-wasting": #1) How bad do you want "It" or need "It"? #2) Are you willing to do what it takes to obtain "It"? #3) Are you willing to do what it takes to maintain 'It" once "It" is obtained?**

Chapter 11
COMMUNICATION

Communication is the key to any relationship: Spiritual, Natural, Business and Personal or otherwise. "Without communication, it is hard to get cooperation or compensation."

"Never discuss your problems with those incapable of helping you to come up with a solution!"

"People make the wrong choices listening to the wrong voices!"-Devin Wyman.

"A Lion never loses sleep over the opinions of sheep."

Always think and use wisdom before you let words fly or spew out of your mouth. Always verify information, proof read and spell-check and/or double-check for errors on any written communication that you send out or print. One wrongly recorded or printed form of communication that gets released can negatively affect you or your image and cause a major or temporary setback.

"10% of most conflict results from a difference of opinion. The other 90% is derived from using the wrong tone of voice or miscommunication."

Chapter 12
STARTING FROM THE BOTTOM WITH LIMITED FUNDS: *"Economics of the nation controls the situation"-Big Ray.*

If you purchased this book and you are working with limited funds/resources to fund your idea, product or service, Pay Close Attention! You must develop alternative sources of income as to where you can generate at least $100+ a day and no less than $50 a day of extracurricular income. This will equate to approximately $1500-3k income per month. You must be willing to invest/save at least 10-20% of this income daily for a year to fuel/jump-start your venture. Go get a separate Savings account/CD to deposit this money in and get in the habit of going to the bank daily {if the bank is closed, deposit it in the ATM or get a separate/additional bank account with a bank that is open 7-days a week. Once you achieve your short-term capital goal, *maintain this habit of investing in yourself and your dreams daily because it will come in handy later on down the line* when you get into acquiring goods & services at volume discounts. **These days**

in America, you need multiple streams of income: A Primary Source; a Secondary Source & "*A-Side Hustle*." Never become totally dependent on just one resource/stream of income because that source could be snatched up or dry up at any given moment & you could become thirsty if you haven't prepared or stocked up for the future. This is a mistake that countless people make. They get a job (*Just-Over-Broke*) with a corporate company or entity where they dangle the carrot or some moderate semblance of success in your face. *If you're good, they will even let you taste the carrot to generate more energy/enthusiasm towards the direction in which they are leading you.* Whenever you take on a job working for someone else, you have to go in with your mindset in the proper perspective that you are there for the purpose of bettering your current situation and know going in that you will not be there forever. Go in with the mindset of **"I am here working for <u>myself/(state your name)</u> at this institution/ business where I have sub-contracted myself or my services as an independent**

representative and I am going to do the best I can where I'm at until I can get to where I want to be." The main gist of this is that **as long as you rely on someone else to make your money you will always be broke** {or paycheck to paycheck}; **You will never get rich working for someone else {only wealthy at best}** and to develop your secondary sources & side hustles while you are working your primary source to prepare for your destiny which is Greatness. In the movie 'Heat", Robert Deniro's character made a statement that was so profound that it stuck with me for awhile: *"Never get so attached to anyone or anything that you can't walk away from in 60-seconds or less and never see again."*

Formulas for Success: A simple saving of $100 invested in mutual funds every month would result in a baby becoming a millionaire by age 20. (Imagine what skipping a snack/soda at the snack machine or better yet buying a snack & soda machine and putting it in a high-traffic/secure location then investing $25 a week in your child's future could do?

Get a product or service that can be mass produced & sold nationwide and/or worldwide of which you can net at least $5+ or more pure profit off of each transaction per unit sold/service rendered. Secure 5 or more channels of distribution (no less than 3) to Market & Promote these products/services nationwide and move at least 10 units minimum per day in each state. This* effort would produce a monthly return of approximately 20k+off of an 8-10 day *work month/approximately 2-2.5 days a week.* **Compare & contrast this to what you would currently bring in working 40+ hours/5-6 days a week for someone else?

***Plug into a Proven Success System and duplicate your efforts. **SYSTEM stands for) Save Your Self Time, Energy & Money!**

'Sometimes you don't need to be a "Rocket-Scientist"; sometimes you just need a Rocket!"-Big Ray

"You don't always have to reinvent the wheel; just paint a new stripe on it with your name on the side!"-Big Ray

Vogue Tire company did this by painting an extra/yellow stripe on a tire, *"nick-named mustard & mayonnaise"* and makes a killing selling these tires to people who want to be different, outstanding or proverbially doing more than the next guy? No knock against the company because their product looks Great and motivates/stimulates the mind of those who purchase them(which makes them a worthwhile purchase because *sometimes in life you have to do what it takes to "jump-start" your enthusiasm regardless of what other people think.)*

-You have to find your "niche." A lot of people knock Multi-Level Marketing (and it's not for everybody) but a lot of people have profited nicely and came up as a result of tying in with the right organization. In most cases they have quality products or services that serve to enhance life, save money & make money. (Look at the countless amounts of success stories of people who were "down & out" and then came up by joining: Amway, Avon, Mary Kay, 5-Linx, Noni, Kiyani, Prepaid Legal, Excel, Visalis, World Ventures, Primerica and countless others?) These businesses usually are a legal and honest side-hustle not to mention the vast amount of new contacts & concepts that you can come across to cross promote/"Piggyback" with your business. Imagine networking & exchanging business cards with a group of pre-motivated individuals at their seminars/meetings and then introducing them to your products & services?   I love getting invited to go to network marketing meetings & seminars because you are going to come into contact with a group of new prospects with an open mind & open checkbooks looking for the next Great Thing-which is YOU!

-SUCCESS Magazine came up strictly off of marketing to Multi-Level Marketing companies.   They "tailor-make" a monthly/quarterly magazine for all of the top-level Multi-Level companies that positions & promotes the individual subscribing company as the best thing going and use them to attract/sign new recruits (unbeknownst to them is that the competing Multi-Level company in the next ballroom has a similar version with their company positioned higher in some other statistical category.

**** *Don't be afraid to do something different or outside of the ordinary to achieve different results! If you are fighting the war on poverty or raising start up capital, you must be willing to use your full arsenal to battle and on other occasions reposition yourself. I have seen some people utilize their personal vehicles to become couriers, delivery people or personal drivers or chauffeurs. I have a relative that does this in a tourist area/major-market and makes approximately $250-600 a night taking people around to their destinations and utilizes the funds to fuel their personal business ventures whenever things get slow. (Look up UBER & LYFT.) On other occasions if you know that you have a good viable business but the fish are not biting where you are located, you may want to reposition yourself or find other lakes, streams, rivers or oceans where the fish are hungry & biting! The same effort used to make a minimum in one market can be used to make millions in another if you will just take your show on the road.*

"The Prophet is without honor in his own town"-Luke 4:24

Chapter 13
MAKE YOUR HEALTH A PRIORITY AND NOT A MINORITY<u>!</u>

"I wish above all things that you may prosper and be in good health even as your soul prospers"-3 John 1:2

"You can have all of the $ in the world, but if you don't have health, you don't have Nothing!"

"Long life is in her right hand; in her left hand are riches and honor."-Proverbs 3:16

Proper Nutrition & Exercise is Essential not only to good health, but to the image & energy that you exude when you present your product & services to others. I remember going to meet an owner of a large internet social media company and while he was having his assistant go over the details of networking with our company with an elaborate power point presentation on his tablet in the hotel lobby of the Hilton, he dropped down and started doing push-ups. That definitely caught my eye. *Many people will go and acquire high dollar material items like houses, boats & automobiles. They will landscape, maintain, wash, & wax it to meticulous standards, fuel it with the choicest premium fuels and oils then go to great detail to make sure these items are insured, secured & garaged to protect their investments but will neglect, misuse ,abuse and under insure their greatest asset which is their body.*

"If you fuel Rolls-Royce dreams with dime-store gas, you will eventually end up on the side of the road waiting for a tow-truck"-Big Ray.

This same thing holds true for your body. Use Wisdom! Proper Maintenance is Essential! If you are going to go out and achieve "Greatness" you will have to be in shape not only to go out and get it but also to bring it back home and to maintain it. Learn about the body plus what makes it click and tick. Once you become a master of your body, you can also become a master of your fate and your soul. Your mind, body and soul need to be able to operate in conjunction with one another in addition to your body being able to perform the tasks that your mind and soul instructs it to do. To maximize your endurance efforts, many publications recommend that you get in 5-6 days a week of cardio exercise & 3-4 days of weight lifting. One program recommended walking/jogging 1-3 miles daily {morning or evening} and working out in the gym 3-4 times weekly while making sure to work the core muscle groups daily. Included in this program was 100(Push-up, Sit-ups & Deep-knee bends daily + the addition of jumping rope 10-sets of 100 daily. Make sure that you stretch properly and hydrate yourself before and after exercising. ***Disclaimer: Check with your doctor before you begin any exercise regimen/program or supplemental products! Furthermore, any supplements, exercise regimens, products or services listed in this publication are for example purposes only, not endorsed by the author or publisher and to be used at your own discretion.***

Chapter 14
READERS ARE LEADERS

"You can tell where a person is going by what he reads."

"Blessed is the man who finds wisdom, the man who gains understanding."-Proverbs 3:13

"Education is the most powerful weapon which you could use to change the world."-Nelson Mandela

"67% of most people that graduate from college never open or read another book in their life." - Dr. George C. Fraser

"The man who does not read good books has no advantage over the man who can't read"-Mark Twain

Start building your "Wealth Library". *Whatever you want to do, or for whatever you want to become, they have a book/books on it!* **Open the book! Read the book!** Utilize the information that can help you and leave the information that can't help you in the book. Just because it can't help you now, doesn't mean that it won't be able to help you in the future when you get up to another level. **The first book that we recommend is a Bible.** It is a life map, unfolds secrets & has answers to every problem known to man. You just have to read, interpret, decipher and **apply the principles within**. Study the Proverbs to obtain wisdom. Make sure you also study up on Solomon, one of the richest men who ever lived. Take note of his success stories and his downfalls and utilize them to your benefit.

*****Special Note:*** *There are several authors that have literature, books and publications that could provide immediate solutions to some of the challenges or obstacles that you may face. Email us for a current list of recommended readings /authors that may assist you in your quest for $uccess!*

Chapter 15
NETWORKING

"If your 5-Closest Friends aren't worth at least $500,000 collectively, then you have a lot of work to do!"- Dr. George C. Fraser

"Your Network determines your Net-Worth!"

Turning Contacts into Contracts! Networking is meeting new people and being able to profit from these contacts. *"Networthing" is being able to profit from these contacts on a consistent/continual basis.* Put yourself in fertile places where networking is matriculating and growth oriented.

People usually spend their money in 7-main areas: Church, Food, Hair, Clothing; Automobiles; Entertainment & Housing! Go where the $ goes & go where the $ grows.

"You usually get what you get around. You can put on a 3-piece suit + nice shoes and go

to work in a barn all day but when you come home, you will smell like horses & hay!"-Big-Ray.

If you're not networking, you're not working! You need to incorporate at least 10-hours bare minimum into your schedule every week towards the guise of networking. As one of your "Success Habits" make it a point to give away at least 5-10 business cards or flyers on a minimum daily which will result in coming into contact with 150-300 new people/contacts/prospects monthly & 1500-3000 new contacts a year of which a certain percentage will subscribe to your theory/products or services. With Success in Life being a Team-Effort and a Numbers Game, this "Success Habit" will help you to reach your goals sooner than just sitting back and waiting on them to come to you. A prominent lady in the Hair industry once told me that *"if you put out 1000 flyers a week, you will never go hungry!"-Joan Louis*

Fertile Places to Network:

*Golf-Courses & Driving Ranges (also try some of the new indoor Golf & specialty places like Top-Golf)

*Gyms & Fitness Centers (Especially chains like 24-Hour Fitness; Lifetime, LA-Fitness)

*Gas Stations/Convenience Stores (QT/Quick-Trip gas stations, 7-Elevens; Circle-K's; Racetrack)

*Wal-Mart's, Sam's Clubs; Costco's; Grocery Store Chains (Whole-Foods; Kroger; Tom Thumb; Albertson's),

Happy Hours at popular Restaurants/Hotels in your city; (Papadeaux, Houlihans, Dugan's; "W"-Hotels, The Omni, The Crowne Plaza, Radisson Hotels, Hilton Hotels; Sheraton Hotels; Embassy Suites; Renaissance Hotels; Hyatt Hotels, Wyndham Hotels

*Little-League Sporting Events, Games & Tournaments: You will encounter mass amounts of people at these events, some of them there for chaperon purposes that are looking for something to occupy their mind until the event is over. One way to tap into the large base of fans that attend these events is to do "giveaways" of products, t-shirts or paraphernalia with your logo & marketing message on it. Another way is to hold drawing for free giveaways where they register/put their name into a drop-box, fish-bowl or ticket spinner.   Don't overlook raffling off big-ticket items for $1- 2 at these events and compiling data off of the ticket stubs.

Compile a List/Database of Customers, Clients & Associates: Make sure that you secure the essential contact info: Proper Spelling of Name, Cell, Email, Mailing Address; Marital Status {name of spouse & kids if any), T-shirts size, favorite color, Birthday and any other demographic information pertinent to your business. As your business grows, this list will prove invaluable in the future.

Chapter 16
UNLEASH THE BEAST WITHIN

In the sports world & the entertainment industry, a "Beast" is described as someone or entity that is dominant in their industry and on top of their game. In the animal kingdom there are various animals which fall under the category of carnivorous {which are meat eaters}. In order to be a "meat-eater", you have to be a natural hunter and sometimes this will require you to be aggressive, intelligent, and strategic, plus a go-getter. In a biblical analogy, it states that

"From the days of John the Baptist until now The Kingdom of Heaven suffereth violence and the violent take it by force". - Mathew 11:12

(Please keep this in proper perspective and realize that the word *"violent"* means aggressive action, not necessarily a harmful act against another.) In the guise of obtaining your goal, sometimes you want to be a force to be reckoned with and at other times be in "stealth" mode and fly under the radar so to speak. As there are various methods to hunt from primitive to next generation, we will describe various attributes of different species in the animal kingdom to tap into for illustration purposes. Some of these will include: **The Lion, Eagle, Guerilla, Shark, and Horse** {not a carnivore). All of these have some similarities as well as vast differences that we want you to tap into & adapt to some of your business principles.

We like *the Lion** because it represents strength and is known as the King of the Jungle. Lions usually hunt in packs which require team-work and they normally have a lot of structure and order in their pride {team or family of lions. Just like the lion, we want you to be the King of Your Craft & get treated like the Royalty that you are! Also, we want you to be able to work in a team-like setting and align yourself with like-minded individuals to achieve your team-goal. Another good thing about the Lion is that it never loses sleep over the opinions of sheep.

*Like **the Eagle** who soars in high places that a lot of other birds can't reach, we want you to soar to higher heights in your endeavors that other people deem unfathomable. Out of all of the birds the Eagle is considered to be the smartest & strongest in addition to being able to fly the highest. The Eagle is highly respected and known for pretty much traveling alone or in pairs and still obtains optimal results in the animal kingdom (Like Navy-SEALS). Sometimes coming up in the Game of Life, you will need to make things happen for yourself, be highly effective obtaining optimal results with little or no help until you can develop your business to the point to where it attracts the kind of people you need on your team to assist. In retrospect, you don't always need a team of people to be successful at what you do; you just need to tap into the Champion within to Succeed. In the sports world, a lot of coaches use the phrase "There is no "I" in TEAM". Our response to this is that there is one in Champion and two in Championship. On the Professional Sports Level (as is also sometimes true in business), "when competition begins, friendship ends". {Perspective point: You always want to have good sportsmanship, play fair and abide by the rules of the game. You have to have character, integrity and principals in whatever arena that you deal in. You never want to develop a reputation of one that plays dirty or uses unfair business practices as this could prove detrimental to long-term business success). One guy used to tell me back when I were in the "hair-industry" that "it ain't no friends in business". Learn to separate Personal from Business. In corporate America we were taught that being a team player comes about after one completes their own assignments. The main gist of this is that you at times have to be able to operate independently of others and still obtain optimal RESULTS! Say to yourself; "If it's to be, It's Up to Me"! Sometimes in Life you have to be a "1-Man (or Woman) Army or Wrecking Crew. A good thing about being an Eagle is that whenever you find yourself in the midst of confusion, chickens, ducks, pigeons or any other animal that eats off of the ground, you can flap your wings a few time and orbit in an atmosphere that smells sweet & is clear.

***The Guerilla** is known for its strength and its magnificent fur. In our world, the guerilla has a duel meaning and is very special.

Google or search the term "Guerilla Marketing" & what it entails and you are about to encompass another world when it comes to obtaining your goals with limited resources and still come out like the King-Kong of your industry. As Denzel Washington's character in the movie training day stated "King-Kong ain't got nothing on me"!

*The reason we mentioned **"The Shark"** is because of its ability to operate swiftly in stealth mode under water and still dominate in its environment. When you enter the water as a human being, you are no longer at the top of the "food-chain" {especially the farther you get from shore or the deeper you get in the water}. When you enter the water of doing business during turbulent times, we want you to be the Hunter and not the hunted, to survive and not get eaten alive. You have to be able to adapt and adjust to any situation or terrain and overcome obstacles to remain victorious!

*The reason we added **the Horse** {even though it's not a carnivore) is because of its size, strength, endurance and ability to go long distances. Another attribute that we like about the Horse is that even though it's not a natural hunter, in the animal kingdom, the horse is not one of the "most-hunted" because of its strength, size, speed and ability to defend itself and fight back with velocity, intensity and power. One blow or kick from a Horse can paralyze or break bones in an adversary. Some of the attributes from the horse that we want you to adapt and to obtain are the ability to go long distances and finish the tasks at hand. Also, even though you may not always be in hunt mode, we want you to position yourself as to where predators know that you are not to be hunted or tampered with due to potential consequences and repercussions.

+In order to be successful, you are going to have to be able to adapt & apply certain attributes of each of the aforementioned animals/Beasts to your game plan at various points along your journey to survive and achieve Greatness!

Chapter 17

3-THINGS WILL GET YOU BEAT IN THIS GAME:
Being Un-disciplined; Un-conditioned and Un-organized!

*Undisciplined: The first step towards Success is Self-Discipline. You want the mind to control the body and not the body controlling the mind. You must discipline and strengthen your mind so that it can send the highest quality signals to the body to operate on your behalf in your best interest. You want your mind strengthened to the point to where it doesn't give in to "temptations of the flesh" and can stay focused on the task at hand to accomplish the goals set forth.

The only reason men fail is due to broken focus. You must target that of which you desire the most and pursue it relentlessly. Learn to eliminate *Distractions, Time-Wasters* & *"Fools"* from your schedule. Phase out those who continually distract you from your focus or goal. Identify *"Time-Wasters"* and *"Fools"* then create a system to protect you from them. *Deny them access to you and any important information.* Anticipate and avoid unnecessary conflicts in addition to never entering into a battle, contest or war where there is no reward. Always remember that a problem on someone else's part doesn't necessarily constitute an emergency on your behalf. Most problems derive from a lack of adequate preparation for the future or bad habits. Keep in mind that Humans are creatures of habit and when put in pressure situations revert back to old habits. Customize your environment to keep yourself focused, motivated & inspired. Create a Daily Success Routine & Habits for Greatness (of which we will go more in depth about in a later chapter).

*Un-conditioned:

"Your lack of conditioning will make a coward out of you"-Jimmy Johnson.

"Fatigue is the Number One Enemy of Your Progress and Joy."-Mike Murdock

"Your ability to deflect pain, inflict pain & withstand pain will sometimes determine the height of your accomplishments."-Big-Ray

You want your body to be in superb shape as not only can you outlast/out-maneuver your opponents but as to where your body can perform like a high-performance race car when your brain sends to it high-quality signals and instructions. Once you learn how to overcome the obstacle of fatigue and increase your endurance, you will notice that your accomplishments & achievements will increase as well {if you put in the work.}

*Being Un-organized: This subject can not only affect your productivity level but your customer/client base and profit margin as well.

"It is better to be prepared for a situation that never happens, than to have a situation happen and not be prepared"-Ron Thompson.

Always prepare adequately for your destiny! This includes knowing where to be and when to be there; arriving on time or before time with adequate knowledge or prior research of the task at hand.

The more organized that you are equates to the more productive you and/ or your business can be in addition to being attractive to potential customers, clients or organizations that could utilize your goods; products or services. You want to organize every facet of your life so that not only everything has a place, but you can be abreast of everything that is going on within your environment and manage accordingly especially in the areas of family, fitness, finance, communication, personnel and security so that you are aware of all activities within to avoid certain pitfalls of life.

Special Note: Organize your schedule to eliminate "Time-wasters" & "Distractions". The time wasted with fools can be invested with Winners!

**Get an Organizer, Desk Calendar or create a daily itinerary of things you intend to accomplish each day & check off completed items. Set alarm reminders on your phone calendars & memo sections as a back-up tool.*

Chapter 18
TRANSPORTATION

"While you were building this business, how were you getting around *"to build"* your Business?"

In many cultures, transportation is directly (and sometimes indirectly) related to: Occupation, Compensation, Cooperation, and Background / Dispensation. A lot of times in an interview process when you are interviewing or reviewing a prospective new employee; associate or a potential new mate the question will often times come up "Do you have reliable & safe transportation?" Transportation not only allows you the ability to get from point A to point B but more so to take advantage of Life's opportunities when they present themselves and to get to the place called *"There!"*

Transportation comes in many shapes & forms (From Buggy's & Horse backs to modern day Cadillac's and on the higher end Mercedes Benz to the vehicle of choice, Rolls Royce) and most times is a direct or indirect reflection of a combination of your personality, mind-set and your position/social status in the life cycle. In your personal life as well as business your transportation can be a part of your branding/ image that you project. Sometimes it's not always about getting from point A to point B but more importantly about the journey and how you arrive! At one point in my career when I was rehabbing from a knee injury and was going to be out for a year from football I went into restaurant management because I eventually wanted to own one and they taught us in training to "start seating customers from the parking lot!" What this essentially meant was to assess the customers as they pulled in according to shape, mode and condition of transportation in addition to their appearance and the number of guests to be seated.

During my under-graduate years as I matriculated in a Business Marketing Curriculum and attended courses such as "Professional-Selling " & Consumer Behavior" we were shown how criteria in regards to a person's vehicle could be used to segment certain parts of a market in addition to indicate certain subconscious buying signs or patterns such as: *A 2-door car indicated more of single or a young person; a 4-door* *car indicated family or team oriented or more committed; The inside of a car reflects how the inside of a person's house is kept; A person who shares their vehicle with more than a mate or family members may be sharing their mate; A person with a vehicle under 5-years old is a good candidate for full-coverage insurance and has or is connected to someone with half-way decent or above average credit; A male's vehicle is a subconscious indicator of his current mate/relationship and sometimes a man who has more than one vehicle for non-business purposes may have more than one mate; A person looking for a new vehicle and their current vehicle is still in great shape may subconsciously be looking for a new mate; A person in a high-end luxury automobile is considered Smart or in a high-end luxury sports car Rich; A guy with a 2-door sports car may be considered to be self-centered or a "player"; A man with a Pick-up truck does manual labor. A man who loans out his car to someone other than close family members or offspring may unconsciously loan out his significant other. A person with a Red vehicle likes personal attention. *As silly as some of* these may sound, you would be surprised as to the variances of criteria that people would use to determine how they approach, treat and serve you.

In certain parts of the country (due to commute, terrain or weather conditions you may find it necessary to have a Back-up or multiple vehicles so that if one goes down you can still move around. You may want to acquire a nice luxury car for when you go out on the town or to go cut deals, an SUV or a Truck with AWD or 4WD for inclimate weather days or for the hauling of groceries or supplies; and for those who commute frequently/long-distances a vehicle that's good on gas mileage. *(Rule of Thumb: When acquiring vehicles for personal use, make sure that each one serves a purpose other than that of ego-boosting. You can only drive one at a time and even if you have reached affluence try to limit yourself to 3-max personal use vehicles. *Also for those that are into" High-end" vehicles look into the option of purchasing pre-owned & leasing new. {The Rule of Thumb is: "If it flies, floats, finagles or drives, Lease it!"} This can save you a considerable chunk of change* *which can be invested or put elsewhere in addition to being a nice tax deduction.*

Maintenance: As with wives/girlfriends, pets, property and portfolios, proper maintenance and attention to your vehicle are essential. Prior preparation prevents poor performance. Keep up with regularly scheduled routine maintenance in addition to making it a habit of keeping your vehicle clean and tidy plus doing a visual & functional inspection of your vehicle every time before you operate it. Utilize Quality Fuels & Oils. Never play yourself cheap. (*Remember that it's a difference between *"cheap" (poor in quality & construction)* and economical (getting maximum quality at the most reasonable price.) Also, when you drive a Benz or any other high-end vehicle and you're trying to win or make ends, you need a friend on your team that specializes in keeping you rolling at the player's price or team rate! Proper maintenance is essential, and when they go down, you still need to get around. Just like in the "Pros" *you can't make the club in the tub"*, **it's hard to get a Win or make a cent if you're not at the event!**

<u>Insurance:</u> For whatever mode of transportation that you choose to travel in (whether car, boat, motorcycle, jet-ski, plane or otherwise) make sure that it is properly insured. When selecting insurance choose wisely and never just let price be the only determining factor. The main value of an insurance policy is not how much you pay, but more-so how it pays off in time of need. Never settle for the industry minimum amount of insurance or just liability (unless your vehicle is valued under $5k). If the industry standard in your state is 25k/50k then bump up to 50k/100k and for those that drive SUV's where most states want you to start off at 50k/100k bump up to 100k/300k of coverage. Be sure to add uninsured motorist coverage and the rental coverage with Roadside Assistance is not a bad option. When purchasing/financing a vehicle make sure that you get "GAP" insurance so that in the event of a total wreck it will cover the difference between the amounts owed to the finance company and the actual value of the vehicle of which the insurance company will pay for. When selecting deductible amounts for your vehicle we recommend the lower

amounts like $500 or under. A lot of times in the case of a mishap, these smaller amounts can sometimes be absorbed by the repair facility & if not, they're easier to come up with in a shorter amount of time than the $750+ & above deductibles.

Special notes on transportation:

Refuse to drive or operate a vehicle that is not insured except in cases of Extreme Emergency/Life or Death Situations! It is better to walk, catch a cab or ride with a friend/ neighbor than to operate a vehicle without insurance and have a mishap occur.

Never loan your vehicle to someone non-related unless it's for business purposes or they are working for you in a business capacity!

Never let someone that is irresponsible or incapable of coming up with the insurance deductible drive or operate your vehicle.

Always do visual inspections of a vehicle before you operate it, especially the tires, fuel & pressure gauges! The Life You Save could be Your Own!

Chapter 19
BUDGETING
"It takes money to make money" & *"A dollar saved is a dollar earned!"*

In corporate America we were taught that most consumers that were experiencing challenges paying their bills were not due to a lack of budgeting, but more so a lack of budgeting correctly. Most consumers failed to consider or encompass all aspects of their lifestyle when creating their budgets. In the Sports World the way that we won games was to come up with a good fundamentally sound game plan to execute that would allow us to score more points than our opponent in addition to limiting our opponent to the fewest points possible. In the "Real-World" or the financial or fiscal arena the way to win is to make or have more $ coming in than that of what you have outgoing. The way to do that is to come up with a good fundamentally sound Budget that will encompass and take care of all of your Needs and allow room for growth on a percentage basis (based upon income & expenses, but yet allow you to save and invest to produce an increase. When creating a budget remember to differentiate between **Needs :(** *those things necessary for day to day survival to stay alive or in business. Re: Maslow's hierarchy of needs.* **, Wants & Desires** in addition to having it flexible enough to adapt and adjust to encompass those "Life-moments" where emergencies do arise. Also make sure that if you are new in business to make separate budgets for home, business & investments (even if they are home based businesses.) You can search the internet and pull up various types of budget sheets and utilize them as a module to create custom budget sheets to fit your lifestyle in relation to debt to income ratio. **Budget Basics:** *Create a budget based upon percentages as to where you can live or operate your business off of 60-70% of your personal/ projected income. Keep your housing costs under 25-35% of income and your transportation costs under 20-25% of income. You want to be in position to tithe 10%, pay yourself 10%, save/ invest 10%+put 5% into an emergency fund & 5% for entertainment purposes. Also for those of you that work a day job or have a corporate career, take advantage of your company's*

401k & company matching program as soon as you start employment. Some companies will match up to 10% on a Pre-tax basis. Utilize this option to get ahead even if your finances are tight in the beginning. For every $100-150 invested on a pre-tax basis, you will only notice approximately a $42 difference in your paycheck. If necessary, skip the snack machine & the cafeteria and bring your own lunch/snacks 2-3 times a week or everyday if necessary. It's a healthier option & more conservative on cash flow.

As an accountant/CPA once told me, "Would you rather pay somebody else in taxes or pay yourself?" If things get extra tight you can always borrow against it twice a year and pay some of your bills up in advance. In addition this option also serves as a nice safety net should you ever unexpectedly get relived of your duties or experience corporate layoffs due to downsizing.

In the business sector (if you own or manage a business) make sure that you allot for overhead & expenses. If starting a "Brick &

Mortar" business from "scratch" (or the beginning stages) make sure that you have enough capital budgeted to cover 12-months of overhead/expenses and no less than 6-months {in addition to asking for the first 2-6 months of rent to be waived for moderations & alterations of dwelling to prepare for opening. Although most people are extremely optimistic & enthusiastic when opening a business in the beginning stages, the reality of the situation is that most "Brick & Mortar" businesses don't start turning a real profit until after 6-12 months of operation. If the dream or the goal doesn't manifest as soon as expected, have enough resources set to the side to fuel the dream or goal until it manifests or matures.

*Special note*Acquire 2-credit cards & build up a limit of at least 2k-10k on each one to have put to the side in case of extreme emergencies or layoffs.

Chapter 20
CREDIT & CREDIBILITY

"A Good Name is far more Precious that diamonds and Rubies"

"Your Credit Score is a gage of your ability to keep your word." –Big-Ray

"CREDIT: Once you get it, don't mess it up!"- Rhonda Hardy

"Don't let your finances be your failure!"- David Mims

"**Credit**" is the root word of "**Credibility**" which is the quality of being "*Trusted*" or "*Believed In*".

One of the definitions of Credit is *"the ability of a customer to obtain goods or services before payment, based on the trust that payment will be made in the future."*

Another one says "*a record of how you have paid your bills in the past.*"

In order for you to come up and get the "*Right*" people on your team and in your corner, you must have "*Credibility*". Unlike "*Image*" which sometimes can or will be a facade or an outward appearance of oneself for business or entertainment purposes, "*Credibility*" deals with the inner man and one's true self. It deals with one's Character, Integrity and Principles in Life.

Most people can't stand a "Liar" {*a person who doesn't tell the truth, can't keep their word or deceives people by leading them astray*} or a "Thief" {*a person who steals or takes from you without your permission or giving back in a proper perspective as agreed upon*}. The same thing holds true with your Credit. A lot of people secure material items with earnest enthusiasm, goods and services based upon good faith and contractual agreement to certain terms, but when the time comes to compensate for these items or services, people catch "*amnesia*" or come up with all kinds of "*Excuses*" for why they can't keep their word {and sometimes have the nerve to catch an attitude when someone tries to hold them accountable for their actions or remind them of the contractual terms of agreement. To stay out of debt and to help keep your credit intact, it is highly recommended that you not only secure the services of a competent financial advisor, but also come up with an *"Emergency Contingency-Plan/Fund"* for those times when *"Life Happens" or* Life's Challenges occur. If your credit is jacked up, do your research on *"Credit Repair"* and get it done. Once you achieve your goal {750+} in this area, use the credit factor in your favor instead of a burden or a pitfall. Protect your credit like you protect your good name and your home.

*** Special Note:** *A moderate $-EMERGENCY CONTINGENCY FUND SHOULD CONSISTENCY FUND SHOULD CONSIST OF THE FOLLOWING:*

$300-1K {Moving & Storage;

$500-INSURANCE Deductible;

$1,200-1,500 EMERGENCY TRAVEL FUND;

$600-1,500 FUNERAL Travel Expenses;

$1,500-2k (Down Payment on New/Used Vehicle in case of Total/ Loss.

$5k-Emergency Legal Expensed/ Bailouts-10%;

+ 2-CREDIT CARDS with $10k credit on them.

+$10k-Emergency Escrow Fund if you own a HOUSE.

***If you don't have an Emergency Contingency Fund, start today by saving $50 a week towards this cause. The headaches that you avoid can be your own.*

Chapter 21
C.Y.A- COVER YOUR ASSETS &
MAXIMIZE YOUR PROFITS WITH THE
4-P's of Marketing

"SELF-PRESERVATION IS THE FIRST LAW OF NATURE!"

This chapter is dedicated to 3-Professors who were very instrumental in my development in addition to inspiring me to Greatness: **Professor Katreece Dyer-Albert** *who taught us that with 1-Good idea, you can eat off of it for 10-years and with 1-Great Idea, you can eat off of it for a Lifetime. She made sure that every student that graduated from the School of Business in Marketing knew what the 4-P's of Marketing were: Product, Place, Promotion & Price,* **Professor Barbara Thomas** *who instilled and taught us certain Principles of Business that if you adhered to them you should stay afloat and survive in even the most challenging of times.* **Professor Earl Marcelle** *taught and prepared us for the "Tricks & Games" that are played in*

Corporate America including the most important concept of C.Y.A.

Cover Your Assets means just that, Protecting Your Most Valuable Assets: Your Name, Your Mind, Your Behind and Your Time! *Entrepreneurship {"Risk Taking"}* as well as *Corporate America {"Trading Time for Money"}* involves a certain degree of challenges and obstacles to be overcome in your pursuit of *"Perceived Happiness"*, Unlimited Earning Potential or "The American Dream". *{As we stated in the book "WINOLOGY: The 48-Laws Of Winning", "Know the Game that You're Playing Before You Begin" and "Adapt and Adjust Your Game to Fit the Terrain".* www.48LawsOfWinning.com

Know your strengths and weaknesses as well as those of your opponents or adversaries then take measures to defend yourself against character attacks, critical judgments in today's highly competitive workplace and potential attempts to sabotage your career by adversaries and "frenemies" alike. For those of you that choose the *Corporate America* route for a career choice or sustenance, *"keep your head on a swivel"* as we say in sports, for someone is always looking to take it off. It used to be a time when people came against you for not doing your job, slacking off or derelictions of duty.   Now-a-days, in today's ultra-competitive work place, People will *"**Hate on You**"* for being productive and doing the job that you were paid to do well or swell. Animosity, Jealousy, Envy and Strive run rampant in today's society, especially in the work environment. The acronym *"**HATERS**"* *stands for "**Having Anger Towards** those* ***Enjoying Real Successes.**"*

Prior   Preparation   Prevents   Poor Performance.

There is a *"Hater"* around every corner and you have to be prepared to deal with them or deal with the consequences of their actions if not defended, diluted or deflected properly. While most *"Haters"* derive from Jealousy, Envy or Strife, people hate for various reasons. Sometimes it may be to your out-performing them or out-producing against them and making them look bad for underachieving or a dereliction of duty. Either way, your perceived performance or Success is Exposing their lack of performance or productivity which may eventually affect their income or employment status if they don't do SOMETHING DIFFERENT or something about it. As they taught us in the Boy Scouts, **"Always Be Prepared!"** Be aware of your surroundings and expect the unexpected in addition to be ready to act or react accordingly. If you are going to work in Corporate America or be in Business period, you need to develop Self-Defense Strategies to combat adversity in today's Highly Competitive Workplace.

Everybody plays an important part in the Ecosystem. *{Utilize haters to their fullest extent while keeping things in their proper perspective to accomplish your goals.* Some of the main reasons that people hate are that they want to be you, be like you or acquire the things that you have. Other reasons may be that "*haters*" are tired of losing while you're Winning or tired of losing to you! (*Read the Chapter on "Turning Haters into Participators" in the book WINOLOGY: The*

48-Laws of Winning
(www.48LawsOfWinning.com}

The 4-P's of Marketing: Product; Place; Promotion & Price.

If you pay close attention to detail of these 4-Principles in regards to developing and marketing your Products, Goods & Services, you will have a Greater Propensity to be Successful in Your Endeavors. A lack of attention or preparation in these areas can result in a loss of market share or an early exit from the marketplace in itself.

PRODUCT) This refers to the Services, items or product offerings that you are attempting to sell or market. When you promote these items or services, it is a reflection of you, the manufacturer and your thought processes at a particular time. Be careful, thoughtful and mindful of these factors and do your research before you accept an assignment or task of marketing or promoting particular products or services, especially if they aren't fully developed or goes against your moral or Religious beliefs or if it doesn't do everything that it's ADVERTISED to do.

AVOID ASSOCIATION WITH *"GET RICH QUICK" or "PONZI"* SCHEMES for *"a Good Name is far more Valuable than Rubies"* and a *"Tarnished"* Reputation is hard to repair.

PLACE) This has to do with channels of distribution and getting the Product to the People or *"The Place Called There".* The Quicker that you get a Product to the Consumer once it has been purchased or Subscribed to, the more satisfied you customer base can be in addition to faster Returns on investment and Higher rates of Customers SATISFACTION. Be particular of your choices of distribution channels for they can reflect "Positively or Negatively" on your image because sometimes it's not always about the Product, but more so the delivery and the way it arrives. Proper packaging & presentation are influential in Consumer purchasing decisions, especially involving Seasonal items.

PROMOTION) Refers to the marketing mediums utilized to advertise or increase Brand Awareness and convince Consumers to purchase or subscribe to your products, goods or services. Remember that Proper Promotion Prevents Poor Performance in Sales and Returns On Investments. Proper Promotion should sometimes include educating the Consumer about product usage & follow up after the sale to encourage CONTINUED patronage of Products, Goods and Services.

PRICE) Pricing structure is an item that has or plays a huge factor in determining the purchase of Products, Goods & Services in addition to what frequency, quantity or amounts are consumed and has a direct correlation to "Supply and Demand" of Products, Goods and Services. Always try to be *"Fair & Equitable"* in your business dealings and as I was taught by my Father to **"Never try to beat somebody out of their money".** Give People Value for their money and they will return. You make money in business by repeat sales & bulk sales.

*<u>**Special Note:**</u> A word to the wise should be sufficient. If you're going to work for a Business or go into Business for yourself, you should educate yourself and prepare for some of the pitfalls and territory that goes along with your particular markets and cross-markets as well. C.Y.A & MAXIMIZE YOUR PROFITS WITH THE 4-P's.*

**: For those of you who choose to accept an assignment or take the "Corporate America"(Trading Time for Money) path for a Career choice, make sure that when you take the job (which stands for "Just Over Broke") that you start preparing and investing for you future by:

1) Having multiple streams of income {A Primary Source, a Secondary Source and a "SIDE-HUSTLE" because you

never know when your Secondary Source may become your Primary means of Survival.

2) *Setting aside 10-20% of your income {in addition to enrollment in the 401k as an "Exit Strategy" to prepare for the day when it's time to leave "the company".*

3) *Have your "Next Job" in your "Back Pocket" in case of "down-sizing", Corporate Lay-Offs, Politics or other Shenanigans.*

4) *Realize that even though a "Job" is what's necessary, <u>ALWAYS be cognizant of the fact that in Corporate America, they can always pull the carpet out from under your feet</u> & if you aren't prepared, you can fall and hit your head on the concrete.*

Chapter 22
CREATE A VISION BOARD & UPDATE IT ON A REGULAR BASIS

"You cannot solve a problem from the same consciousness that caused it. You must see the world anew."-Albert Einstein

Create a Vision Board to keep your Goals, Dreams and Aspirations alive & motivated. In the Bible there are parables that make reference to *"Without a vision the people shall perish"* and *"Write the vision down and make it plain to see,..."* (Habakkuk 3: Your vision board should illustrate & encompass parts of your game plan, mid-range and long-term goals in addition to pictures or illustrations of things that you want to acquire and where you want to be in the future. As you develop your business entity, your marketing mix and promotional mediums will encompass some of these things on your vision board to stimulate new growth in business. In a Marketing curriculum we were taught that "visual is 93% of your presentation".

"Finally brethren, whatsoever things are true, whatsoever things are honest, whatsoever things are just, whatsoever things are pure, whatsoever things are lovely, whatsoever things are of good report; if there be any virtue, and if there be any praise, think on these things."-Philippians 4:8

"Where there is no vision, the people shall perish..."-Proverbs 29:18

*In order to win or acquire the "Big-One" you must first visualize and see yourself accomplishing this task.

"So as a man thinketh in his heart, so is he."

You must have a mind to Prosper and a Will to Win.

"Life is not made up of "the haves" and "the have-nots", but more so "the wills" and "the will-not."-Big Ray

The only reason men fail is due to broken focus. You must target that of which you desire the most and pursue it relentlessly.

Don't let the opinions of the average man sway you. Dream and he thinks you're crazy. Succeed and he thinks you're lucky. Acquire wealth and he thinks you're greedy. Pay no attention, He simply doesn't understand. Complaining people focus on the wrong things. *If you're going to be "King of the Jungle", remember that Lions never lose sleep over the opinions of sheep.* Happiness is not an accident, nor is it something you wish for. Happiness is something you design! Never depend on someone else for Love and Happiness. Love yourself and be happy to be breathing.

"In Jesus Name I Win, in the game of Life, AMEN!"

*Anticipate and avoid unnecessary conflicts in addition to never entering into a battle, contest or war where there is no reward.

Chapter 23
ADAPT AND ADJUST YOUR GAME TO FIT THE TERRAIN

"Never make a Long-Term decision based upon a temporary situation."!

"When you're born or operating in a jungle, there is no such thing as "Crawl before you walk?' You have about 15-18 minutes to get it together when you exit the womb, and then you have to hit the ground running or get left behind!"-Big Ray

"Being Challenged in Life is inevitable. Being defeated is Optional!"-Roger Crawford

"You must either modify your dreams or magnify your skill"-Jim Rhone

Anticipate that there will be obstacles along your journey towards "Greatness" that will have to be solved, resolved or overcome in order for you to reach and achieve your

Goals & Objectives. Due to the competitive nature of Life, you will mainly encounter 4-types of people & you will have to figure out which one are you: *Those who make things happen; those who watch things happen, those that wonder what happened & those that things happen to!*

I grew up in the Midwest) Detroit, Michigan aka *"The Murder-Capital of The World"*

"Where the Strong Survive and the rest get eaten alive!"

 It was a nice place to go shopping for cars, suits & shoes, but you did not want to live there. Growing up we learned fast that in order to be successful; you had to be able to overcome obstacles quick and to **"adapt & adjust your game to fit the terrain."** *Not only did we have to deal with the elements (The 4-Seasons), but We Had to Deal with "The-Elements" (Day-to-day Survival/Staying Alive! For most residents, operating in "Fear"* **(False Evidence Appearing Real)** *was* not an option if you planned on staying or living a victorious lifestyle? For those who did, their future was not in Detroit. Close encounters with Bully's, Robbers, Muggers;

Thugs, Thieves & Con-men were commonplace even in the more affluent areas of town. You couldn't always run from it (unless you relocated to another state & sometimes they still came and found you) because a lot of times you would encounter the same problem the next day in your daily commute or on your journey to school. As the singer Kenney Rogers stated & sang in the movie *The Gambler:*

"You have to know when to hold them, know when to fold them, know when to walk-away and know when to Run! "

(In my family, the only time running from people or your problems were acceptable was in the case of someone shooting at you or bullets flying. Other than that, you had to handle your business or you were going to get the Business!)

At a very early age, we developed gifts of discernment, networking, assessment & problem solving skills in addition to learning how to barter, communicate & negotiate! Tasks that seem simple to most such as going to school or to the store to pick up items for your parents were challenging and required a certain degree of preparation (Like going to war). I've heard several stories of kids getting sent to the store (or school) & getting jumped or robbed in the process and returning home empty-handed or minus an article of clothing or shoes.   Once their parent or guardian got wind of the situation, they would give them a *"motivational speech"*, sometimes a whipping and a set of instructions along with cash & tools to complete the task or rites of passage and told not to return to the house without the items they were sent for or with. *(Back in those days, the only acceptable excuse for coming home empty-handed was if someone pulled a gun on you or was shooting at you!)* It's a Jungle out there and Situations such as these cause you to mature at a rapid rate and come up with solutions to problems that present themselves in a matter of minutes, sometime seconds to alleviate having to deal with a larger problem later on. *"Imagine being young and experiencing a robbery/mugging then being faced with the possibility of homelessness if you didn't retrieve the lost or stolen items?"* This would definitely put you in a different frame of mind! You find out quick how to win/ beat someone or alleviate & eliminate problems and incorporate it into your game-plan. The **9**-main ways that you beat an opponent is to: **#1-HAVE GOD ON YOUR SIDE; Overpower them** (Dominate Your Opponent & annihilate their will to win), **Out-Quick them**(Run-Faster, Get the jump on them/Be First or Beat them to the Punch), **Out-Think them** (Strategy/Come up with a Better Game-Plan than theirs or find their weakness and exploit it), **Out-Last them**(Endurance/You're in Better Shape or able to withstand the conditions longer than they can. *"You'll Win if You Don't Quit!"*) **The Element of Surprise-"Catch Them Slipping, Sleeping or Leaking"** (Sometimes when an opponent doesn't respect you or see you as a potential threat to defeat them, they will get lacksidasical, sloppy or complacent with the status-quo and let their guards down or prepare inadequately which would make that a prime time for a counter-attack. **Join Them** (*"Sometimes if you can't beat them, join them"* Sometimes you have to infiltrate an opponent's camps, study & scout them out to determine what their mindset, theories, strengths, weaknesses , common enemies, common allies and utilize this information to your best benefit. ***Other times, if you can't beat them "Hire Them."*** Some people are just good at what they do and are a technician or master of the game. With you wanting the Best possible Team, Product or Service available, why not tender an offer to that adversary that has proven to be a major challenge or stumbling block in your path or pursuit of Excellence. Sometimes, what the competition/ opposition was doing wasn't personal, just business and if this is the case, tendering an offer that they can't refuse will help to overcome a challenge in addition to improving productivity in just one move. Sometimes grass can be greener on the other side of the fence if the right seeds are planted, watered and fertilized. **Relocate to an area or environment where the adversary would become inefficient or ineffective.** Every challenge in life doesn't always have to be a "Battle or a War." Sometimes it works better to *"think smarter instead of harder."* Just as in business Location plays an important part, proper positioning can not only serve useful in marketing, branding & promotional terms but be a major security mechanism as well. Just as in the scientific arena where *Geography determines growth*, or even the plant & animal kingdom where certain organisms needs certain elements, climate or type of environment in order to survive, feed or feel comfortable, the same holds true with the opposition. Prime examples; fresh water fish don't do well in salt water & vice versa; certain fruits & vegetables don't grow well or go bad in certain climates; certain animals, mammals or man can't survive well at lower depths of the sea without proper protection or a pressure suit because of the variances of air pressure at certain depths; when you go up the side of a mountain, they have a snake line. Snakes can't survive at higher altitudes because of the atmospheric pressure on their brain. *In retrospect, "Let your next move be your best move like a chess move!" A simple move up the mountainside, into the suburbs or the countryside can not only reduce the competition but sometimes create a position of attractiveness, affluence and of a monopoly {which depending on the type of business that you are in + the supply & demand for your product or services is not always a bad thing.*

Eliminate the Threat(Sometimes in Life as in Business you have to put opponents out of business or into early retirement (*legally or through fair competitive practices*)or rearrange their focus to things that are more important than competing with you! Very Important: Before you try using this measure use Wisdom and don't be Greedy because it's enough out here for everybody. *Everybody plays an important part in the ecosystem*. If you eliminate all competitors this would create a situation of a monopoly after which would make you a target and sooner or later someone will try to use this measure on you? (*There is more than one way to skin a cat! Sometimes you may want to leave a couple of "small-fries" or cats in business so that they can take care of the "rats" or undesirables that you choose not to do business with.*)

Dealing with the elements: When I was a Boy Scout, our motto was "Always Be Prepared!" Growing up in the Midwest we encompassed all 4-seasons of weather that included snow, ice, rain, heat, fallen leaves, strong-winds & tornados. When the seasons changed, we changed and or adapted to fit the terrain that came with each new season. At the end of August we might be wearing Bermuda shorts, flip-flops & tank tops. By the 3rd week of September you had better have a windbreaker, sweater or light jacket available to fight off the brisk winds of autumn approaching. Entering into the 2nd or 3rd week of October when the cold fronts were more prominent we started breaking out with the dress boots & mid-weight sweaters or leather coats & jackets. When December arrived, it was time to break out the snow boots & ski suits along with the heavyweight parkas and overcoats. Towards the end of March –the middle of May it was time to break out the active "Rain-gear'. June signaled the time to break out your lightweight linens and open toe shoes or sandals.

In the Sports World sometimes we would be going up against a formidable opponent that had very talented athletes and still had to find a way to accomplish our goals and come out victorious.

"It's not the amount of times that you try, but more so the means by which one is willing to go through to reach their objective!"

Our mission was to get their star players (or difference makers) to lose focus and turn their attention span to something other than winning against us by any means necessary. Some of the tactics used to accomplish this task were mental such as silly prank phone calls the night before the game or talking trash to an opponent during and in between plays. Other tactics were obstacles such as not cutting the grass & watering it extensively with a fire hose or physical such as "Gang-tackling" an opponent & hitting them extra hard under the pile or setting hard picks, fouls or screens.

In the Business world sometimes we run specials, discounts & give-a ways or somewhat slanderous commercials to get opponents/competitors to lose focus.

From my observations and experiences, one of the quickest ways an opponent would lose focus was in the event of "Pain!"

"Pain changes the Game!"-Big-Ray

Pain can come in many shapes and forms: Physical, Mental & Financial.

"Your ability to deflect pain, inflict pain & withstand pain will sometimes determine the height of your accomplishments."-Big-Ray

"Everybody has a plan until they get hit!"-Mike Tyson

Sometimes in life in order to repel an opponent or an adversary you have to administer a "blow"*(message)* so shocking, intense and convincing that your adversary will have to revaluate & refocus their reasons for competing against or trying to suppress your efforts in the first place? *(When you deliver this blow it has to be with a high-level of intensity so that your opponent is "Convinced" that you are not the one to be toyed with! Now whether you decide to deliver this message to their mind, behind or bank-account or all 3-at the same time is up to you! If you come with anything less than intense this method will back-fire & you should prepare to receive a barrage of retaliation!*

Choose Not to Lose! "Winning is a Lifestyle"!

*The moral to the stories are that sometimes situations & circumstances force you to adapt & adjust to overcome obstacles, challenges & fears to find a way to Survive or Win!

Special Note: Keep things in proper perspective! *Stories mentioned in this book are for illustration & motivation purposes only!* **Do not misconstrue the contents of this book or the intentions of the author as those of inciting illegal activity or violence towards another human being! Life is a Precious Gift from GOD! Do whatever you can to preserve and enjoy it while it last! "Self-Preservation if the First Law of Nature!" Protect Yourself at All Times!** *Regardless of your situation or* *circumstances all things in life are temporal/ temporary and* **you can Win if You Don't Quit!** *Find the Champion up above & within, because* **CHAMPIONS ALWAYS FIND A WAY TO WIN!**

Chapter 24
THE GAME IS TO BE SOLD,
NOT TO BE TOLD!

*This Chapter is intended to help you keep things in "Proper Perspective."

The "*Game*" refers to whatever your "*Livelihood*", "*Specialty*", "*Gift*" or area of Expertise is. This Chapter is specifically intended for Professionals and those in Business or Business Ownership, because **most people go into Business to Make Money** and **Professionals "*GET PAID*" Consistently!** *Amateurs DON'T*! Amateurs, this chapter may not be for you {until you're ready to Change Your Status} even though "*Everybody Plays an Important Part in the Ecosystem.*" The Only thing "*FREE*" in this world is "*AIR*", "*OPPORTUNITY*" &"*SALVATION*" {because they are selling water by the bottle and oxygen by the tank. On the back of your dollar, it states "***IN GOD WE TRUST*" in Bold Letters.** When you get to reading and interpreting some of the foreign language on the back of that same dollar, you will come to find out that "**All others must pay!**" Have you ever stopped to ask yourself "**Why does the currency in a country whose primary language is English have inscriptions & decryptions on it in languages that are mainly un-interpretable with common knowledge?**" The system is designed to lead you astray and for the "*Rich to get Richer*" and the Poor to be just that. Unless you educate yourself and get knowledge on the purpose and processes of money being a medium of exchange, a lot of times, it will pass you by. The Bible says that "*my people perish for a lack of knowledge...*"-Hosea 4:6 {some translations state "are destroyed" instead of "perish".

If you're in Business or a Professional, there is nothing wrong with annual or semi-annual giveaways, having loss-leaders or giving away samples, promotional items or "*Test-Drives*" to attract and bring in "*New-Business*" nor having "*Referral based incentives*" to reward, motivate and inspire your current clientele or workforce, but *you* *can't give away the whole business*. **People don't Respect "*FREE*"** unless it's "*Gift Wrapped*" or in a "*Sponsorship*" package. The only time "*telling your business*" is acceptable is when its work related in the guise of advertising, marketing or prospecting for new business & clients or offering the opportunity to become a part of your business for expansion & growth purposes. The Bible makes reference to "*All hard work leads to profit, but mere talk only leads to poverty*"-*Proverbs 14:23* & "*Do not muzzle the ox when he treadeth the corn and the servant is worthy of his hire*"- *1Timothy 5:19*

In the **Sports realm**, if you're at a place where they're not "*buying in*" to your programs, theories, systems or analogies; don't give it away for free. Just because it's not valued in a particular market or region, doesn't mean that you information is not Valuable. "One man's trash is another man's Treasure." Sometimes you have to take your show on the road and "Go where you're celebrated and not where you're tolerated!"

The Bible makes reference to *"A prophet is not without honor except in his own town and his own home"* (Mark 13:57; Mark 6:4; Luke 4:24

Even in the guise of the **Educational Process** which includes ***"Acquired"* knowledge & *"Bought"* knowledge**. Acquired knowledge is usually obtained through experiences, situations and circumstances. Bought knowledge is usually acquired through privileged information, higher or specialized education processes, seminars or workshops & literature. In the common vernacular, you may hear references to **being *"taught"* & *"schooled?"*** Translation- When you have been *"taught'*, it was because you were educated or trained in reference to a certain topic or subject matter. When you hear the terminology about being *"schooled"*, this refers to learning a lesson from experience or sometimes from having been fooled in some area or another due to lack of knowledge.

A lot of times people don't learn to appreciate *"Education"* or start to take it seriously until it costs them something, they have to pay for it or they are *forced to "Learn" due to situations and circumstances*. A prime example of this is Public School, Private School and College Education. A lot of people take the Public School Education for granted because it's a Right and everyone is entitled. Now, when you transition over to Private School Education, you have qualifying criteria for acceptance and the "Privilege" of attending and for the most part, it's going to cost you something unless you're a "special case" and you're doing a trade off for *"goods & services."* Now when you get to the College Level, almost everyone has to pay unless you're on Scholarship and bringing something to the table other than a *"derriere and a smile."*

The main Reason You Go to College is to *"Learn How to Make Money"* or become "Professional" or "Certified" to make Money. What they don't tell you is that you don't have to wait until you graduate to start making money. Even in an *"Amateur"* or *"Novice"* status, there are ways to **make your learning process or experience *"Profitable"*, "Rewarding" and Mutually**

Beneficial.   Keep in mind the words "**Supply & Demand**" and that the way you make money is by displaying your "*gifts*", finding your "***niche***" and **solving problems for others**.   {*Read Proverbs 18:16 & Ecclesiastes10:19*

Another scenario in the Educational Process is that **Education is a Business** and *according to the level of your education, where you were educated and by whom you were instructed will have a direct bearing on how you are viewed, received and rewarded by society.* A lot of people don't understand the "perceived Value" of an Education and have a hard time or are averse to paying for the "Power" that the information, associations & connections that education provides. Ask yourself what is the price of getting educated at **Hampton, Harvard, Howard or Stanford** *versus the variance in costs and prestige from getting educated at your local community college or State school?* Life is about Choices. **Choose Not to Lose!** In Life, you will make some Good Decisions and some not so good decisions of which there may be consequences and repercussions.

"Study to show thyself approved unto God, a workman who needeth not to be ashamed, rightly dividing the word of truth"-2 Timothy 2:15

"The instructions that you follow, will determine the future that you create"-Mike Murdock

In **Corporate America**, they will dangle that apple, carrot; trinket or dollar in your face to **sell you the *"Dream"* of Living Life Happily Ever after** to keep you motivated and inspired to make them as much money as possible. What they don't tell you is that if you utilized 20-30% of the effort with the *"same enthusiasm"* that you exhibited in the corporate sector into your own business, you could bring in the same amount or more working your own business and developing your own Empire. The sad part about this is scenario is most people "can't handle the truth" or don't want to face these facts until after they have invested 10-20 years of their lives into the dream of corporate America and have exhausted a large portion of their "youthful exuberance" or energy needed to kick off a business of their own. When you go into corporate America, you have to **go in with a "*Game plan*"** whether it is a 3yr, 5yr or 10yr plan to get in, stack your "paper", learn the systems and make valuable connections **to be utilized in future endeavors.** Do not get comfortable or complacent because they can and sometimes will pull the carpet out from under your feet and you have to be prepared to land correctly when this situation arises.

In Relationships, realize that **GOD *sends people into your life for a Reason, a Season or a Lifetime*. "*People will come and go.*"** It is up to you to **realize as to what "*intent*" that people have come into your life for and fully utilize them to that extent**. Some people will tell you that it's not right to use people? I'm going to tell you that people are a resource to be utilized to achieve your goals and aspirations, but it's not alright to "*misuse*" people. Always be fair in your business dealings and personal relationships.   Realize that **relationships are a process of exchange and sometimes dissolve when they are no longer mutually beneficial** or the exchange dissipates. A lot of times people forget that whatever it takes to acquire or engage in a certain situation or entity is also sometimes necessary to remain in place to maintain that same situation or entity. Change is inevitable.   Sometimes you embrace change and other times, change is instituted upon you.   Things change and people change. ***"Dating"* consists of gather data to see if you want to continue to journey farther in the same direction with a person or entity** or change pathways. **When or if that time ever comes to part ways have or create an *"Exit strategy* "**and make every attempt to do so peacefully and amicably.   Life is about "*Choices*", **Choose Not to Lose!**   If they're not for you, "*clean & clear your plate or slate*" & "*get rid of excess baggage*" so you can have room for the next one or the "*Chosen-1*" that is supposed to be there. **Time is a Valuable Commodity which once lost can never be regained**. **Never**

spend "Major Time" with minor people unless they are *"paying like I'm weighing"* for your goods, products or services.

Be cognizant of the fact that every situation is not for you and if it's not on the path between you and your goals, it's not for you to deal with and May often times be a distraction. Don't be quick to jump into "New Relationships" too fast without giving it considerable thought. *A lot of times the first 60-90 days of a "New Relationship" are all a front or a façade and most of the time, you're just dealing with their "Representative."* Use patience and wisdom to save yourself a lot of headaches, time and trouble.

"Before You come out of Your Pocket and Spend a "dime", You had better strategize and use your mind"-Big Ray

Learn to eliminate *"Time-Wasters"* and get yourself a **"SYSTEM"** {*which stands for* **"Save Yourself Time, Energy & Money"**} to **eliminate, block & lock "Time-**

Wasters", "Fools" and *those who don't Respect Your Time or your dime* from your schedule.

Special Note: Everything is not always a "hustle" or about a dollar, even though it's amazing that even in the amateur arena, they want you "hustling & humping" at a fast pace for free. Don't be afraid to donate and give back to them that have helped you to come up along the way or from where you have received, especially to the communities in which you live to help make society a better place in addition to helping today's youth develop on a positive path so that you don't have to deal with them in adverse situations later in life.

**Special Note: Organize your schedule to eliminate "Time-wasters" & "Distractions". The time wasted with fools can be invested with Winners! "The Quickest Way to get Defeated is to become Distracted".*

*** ***The Breakdown:*** *Imagine that you have your own personal Kingdom and Sanctuary available to you fully equipped with all of the items and ambience to keep you "Happy" & "Satisfied". Now Picture yourself as a "King" or "Queen" of this Wonderful Kingdom & Sanctuary and think of some creative means to describe your "Kingdom & Sanctuary" in addition to whom you would allow access and why? To begin with, let's start off with the names. Since we don't do "magic", we will call it "Miracle" Kingdom; and due to the fact that "Magic Kingdom" is owned by "Disney World", we won't' call it "Disney's World"; we will call it "Your World." As for whom you would allow "Full" or "Direct" access, it would more than likely be those who are in your "Inner-circle" or on "Your Team". Now close your eyes and visualize on this "Miracle Kingdom" in "Your World" for a minute or two before I come back to you with some "News that you can use" plus information and concepts to enlighten your experience.*

Knowledge is the new "currency" and access to Information equates to "Power." *Sometimes access to information on "the Game" can be bigger than "the Game" itself, because playing "the Game" or being a "Player" in "the Game" can sometimes have an "Expiration" date. When you take ownership or have dominion over information on "the Game", now you can position yourself to profit and prosper from it for a Lifetime and for generations to come after you're gone. Ask Walt Disney and Al Davis.*

Now back to the Kingdom at hand: **"Miracle Kingdom" in "Your World".** *If you spent time, energy, efforts and resources to develop and build an Empire (The "Miracle Kingdom" in "Your World", why would you take and give the "Blue-Prints" + Recipes for Success in your "Miracle Kingdom" or "* **Power"** *over "Your World" to someone non-associated or not on your Team without being compensated?* **If you owned "Disney World" or "McDonald's" would you give it away for free or Charge**

admission and Franchise it out? *If you give it away for free, how long do you think it will last and where do you think you would end up?*

FOOD FOR THOUGHT!

Chapter 25
CREATE A DAILY SUCCESS ROUTINE AND HABITS FOR GREATNESS:

"You cannot change your Life until YOU CHANGE YOUR HABITS!"

"You are what you repeatedly do. Excellence therefore is not an act, but a habit"-Aristotle

When you perform an act for 21-days straight it becomes a habit. When you continue with this new habit for 40 days or more, it now becomes a Lifestyle! (Google Search: "Winning is a Lifestyle")

<u>"Success Habits"</u>

***KEEP GOD FIRST, Because HE'S GOING TO BE FIRST* ANYWAY**!

"Seek ye first the kingdom of GOD and his righteousness and all these things shall be added unto you"-Mathew 6:33

If GOD isn't in it, don't accept the task/assignment or job regardless of how much it pays because it won't last long!

Learn to Value Your Time! Time is a valuable commodity which once lost can never be regained! The main difference between the poor and the wealthy is the value they put on their time. Don't waste it. Get a good concept of time and fully utilize it to that extent.

*Always take care of Home! *Never get so caught up in the Business or outside world as to where you neglect or forget the real reason **"Why"** you are doing this in the first place. Home is where the heart is. If home isn't taken care of in all aspects, either you are doing too much or not enough! **In addition to taking care of home, make sure that you have adequate security mechanisms (including hidden cameras/microphones) in your home, business, office & transportation**. They now have the systems where you can check your home, vehicle or business from the other side of the world via cell phone, tablet or computer. Remember the root of Security is: "Secure-it." A word to the wise should be sufficient! Also as you ascend the ladder of affluence make sure that you have an "armor bearer" on the team/speed-dial or someone* *that can double in that capacity until you develop a need to acquire personal or executive security. (Ex-College football players serve well in this capacity. Not only are they educated and have the physique, but a team concept as well.*

"Never discuss your problems with those incapable of helping you to come up with a solution!**"*

****Study to show thyself approved!** To master your game, you must first become a student of the game. Whatever you want to become, whatever you want to achieve, accumulate or acquire they have a book on it. "Study to show thyself approved." Readers are leaders and the reason why is because they are ahead of the game in reference to knowledge & application of that knowledge. The Bible says that the people shall perish for a lack of knowledge. This passage holds true in various facets of life: Spiritual, Social, Physical, Financial, Business and Relationships.*

****Always stay abreast of/ be aware of the competition & the position of the***

enemy. They are in business to put you out of Business (or take your head off)!

Turn Contacts into Contracts: *Make it a point to give away at least 5-10 business cards or flyers on a minimum daily which will result in coming into contact with 150-300 new people/contacts/prospects monthly & 1500-3000 new contacts a year of which a certain percentage will subscribe to your theory/product or service. With Success in Life being a Team-Effort and a Numbers Game, this "Success Habit" will help you to reach your goals sooner that just sitting back and waiting on them to come to you.*

Campaign Like You're Trying to Make the Hall of Fame! *"If you put out 1000+ flyers {or business cards} a week, you will never go hungry"-Joan Louis. {When people hear your name, they need to know who you are and that you're Good at what you do!*

Be detailed oriented. *It's the little things that count!*

*Don't be afraid to ask questions. They told us in football that the only dumb question is the un-asked question.

Don't Expect What you don't Inspect! *Game-Test to Bring out The Best!* Always check important items going out to customer's clients & prospects by having a second person double check the items prior to shipping or delivery. *(People always act differently when you are watching them. Create a "Checks & Balance" System so that not only your business but everything that goes out of the door is double-checked for consistency, quality & clarity. This can help to eliminate problems & reduce challenges before they occur.)* Know your personnel and keep in constant contact. *Always know what's going on in all aspects of your business, financial & personal life + the current trends in your industry.* *Regardless of the arena or entity, whether Military; Sports; Corporate America; Personal Relationships or Private Enterprise, you must "Game-Test" all applicants/prospects to show Position worthiness and Battle readiness. Prime example: In the military they have specialized training exercises, mock wars and battlefield simulation operations to gauge the quality of response, aptitude and performance. In sports they have what they* call scrimmages against each other and against simulated opponents to evaluate talent & potential to operate under stress, duress and game like situations. In the school system they have fire drills. In the public sector they have tornado drills/air-raid sirens. In the media they have news-flashes/public-service announcements. In personal relationships you must "Game-Test" potential mates to make sure that they are not "star-struck" or" fair-weather fans" and in it for the long-haul & not just for short-term benefits or for entertainment purposes.

* Don't make your Priorities a Minority! Get an Organizer, Desk Calendar or create a daily itinerary of things you intend to accomplish each day & check off completed items. Set alarm reminders on your phone calendars & memo sections as a back-up tool.

*Customize your environment to keep you motivated & inspired.

*Prepare for Your Destiny.

*Stay Clean & Keep Good Hygiene.

If you want to be Great, Surround Yourself with Greatness on a Regular Basis!

Be careful of the company you keep! Sometimes people assume by association & image means a lot.

* Write a Book on whatever you're Good at and leave a legacy. Don't let your history be a mystery. Remember "the game is to be sold, not to be told and when you sell it, make sure that you (and everybody associated) gets their cut/fair-share!" Not only does becoming an author put you in a select segment of society, it legitimizes your projects in addition to positioning you as an expert at what you do. Your book can go places that you can't go in addition to opening doors that were previously inaccessible.*

Make Everyday Payday whether you're working or not. Find out what Residual Income is. Also living paycheck-to-paycheck is alright as long as its daily paychecks!

Dress for Success! Look The Part and Play The Part!

Always Put Yourself in Position for Recognition!

"It's better to make the News than to be the News!"-Big Ray

When opportunities present themselves to establish your good name, integrity & reputation, seize the moment. A good name and reputation is more powerful than money. (Proverbs 22:1) Basically what we are saying is to provide things honest in the sight of all men and always be productive. This is not a statement to go out & toot your own horn (Proverbs 27:2) but more so to give people value for their money and never try to beat someone out of their money. Your gifts & talents will make a way before great men.

Learn to Eliminate Time Wasters and get rid of those that don't respect your time or your dime!

*Do Not Be Afraid to Walk Away from Mediocrity when it is an accepted practice and the majority present are unwilling to change.

*Treat Loyalty Like Royalty! *As my mother always said "Good Help is Hard to*

Find!" When you find someone that's loyal to you and not just liking you for your paper or the things that you can do, take the time as often as possible to reward and let that person know that they are very much appreciated. You will definitely find out who your true friends are when you lose the limelight or things get tight! It's always good to have Good People on Your Team! You never know when you are going to need them to make a play?

*Remember that Business & Personal Business don't always mix! Unless you're married or closely related or If it's not a family owned business, keep your business and your family totally separated until it's time to bring an offspring up and teach them how to take over the business. Only those closest to you can hurt you (and it's often harder to retaliate or take legal action against a relative because you might be the same one having to bail them out or pay their hospital bill!)

*Get an intro-song/theme song or a gospel hit that makes you feel Great and play it anytime you don't feel on top of your game!

*Learn how to play Golf. A lot of deals and quality contacts are made on the Golf-course. A hidden attraction is that this is a game that requires participants to be honest, possess integrity and have Self-discipline because of the lack of a referee. Imagine how many relationships and financial transactions would have lasted longer and been stronger had the parties involved possessed the aforementioned qualities/traits?

*Walk at least 1-3 miles daily & Brainstorm during these walking sessions.

*Always carry a mini-digital recorder with you at all times to take notes on any ideas you may come up with while they are fresh on your mind.

* Go where the $ goes & go where the $ flows & grows! **People usually spend their money in 7-main areas: Church, Food, Hair, Clothing; Automobiles; Entertainment & Housing! You should have your hand, your ear and your marketing message in at least 4 or 5 out of the 7?** It is a given that a majority of people are always going to Praise GOD, need something to eat, need a haircut or style;

need something to wear, someplace to stay & Transportation.

*Don't be afraid to ask for "Quality" referrals from family members, friends, customers & clients. Remember that a closed mouth rarely gets fed!

Train the people that you delegate tasks to do the things the way you like them done. Hire for attitude & train for aptitude! As a business owner or leader you are always constantly evaluating the people who help to achieve team goals. If you have people on your team who aren't willing to work to improve the team, help the team reach its goals or to bring in new business, you should evaluate why they are still with your team or business?

*Get a competent mentor who is successful in your field.

*Don't waste your vote.

Protect Your Name! It is going to outlast you!

*When contemplating entering into new interpersonal relationships have a pad with at *least 25+ or more qualities listed that you are looking for in a mate then grade out/pre-screen new applicants on a percentage basis of how they stack up against your list to eliminate wasting your time, their time or your dime! (If you didn't have at least 20-25 preferred qualities listed, you didn't give it much considerable thought & go back and think thoroughly. They should grade out at) 70% or more to be your friend; 80% or more to be a girlfriend/boyfriend & 90% or better for marriage material.)   Nobody is perfect, but there is someone perfect for you! This eliminates having to go through 9 or 10 candidates just to find out number 4 was the right one!*

*Develop your craft and become a Specialist or a Technician at what you do!

*Remember: The Golden Rule! *In elementary or pre-school you were lead to believe that the Golden Rule meant to do unto others as you would have them to do unto you in order to create a cooperative atmosphere of peace, order, tranquility and non-violence toward others. Fast-forward years later to post-adolescence; where you* start experiencing the "Real-World" that is "Cold, Cruel & Cut-throat" with chaos and not so nice actions going on which out the true revelation of the meaning of this term. {Treat others like they need to be treated according to their actions & productivity and to remember that he who has the gold, rules.

*Go Where You are Celebrated & not where you are tolerated!

***PAY YOUR TAXES!** A guy named "Uncle-Sam" (who is probably not related to you) has to get his cut of whatever it is that you may be making even though he didn't help you to earn it. As bad as it may sound, it can get worse because if he doesn't get his cut and he finds out, he will send his 3-letter cousins "the alphabet-boys" to come collect it for him & it won't be nice! Consider taxes as one of your costs of doing business & pay them up front or on a quarterly basis so that you don't have to come up with a lump sum at the end/beginning of the year.

* Follow a Plan and not a man (nor a woman.)

*Become a Lifetime Enjoyment Specialist!

Keep at least 10 millionaires on speed-dial in your phone: They have connections and access to people, products & services that other people can only dream about. Remember *"Team-work makes the Dream Work"* & the acronym *T.E.A.M stands for Together Everybody Achieves More!* One of the Best Motivating Factors that you can have in Business is Financial Backing! Also keep in mind that a lot of people with resources are always looking for good opportunities to multiply their reserves, gifts & talents with minimal effort. (*VERY IMPORTANT: Always Use WISDOM & Make sure that before you approach someone asking to utilize their hard earned $ & contacts that you have thoroughly researched & game-tested your idea or proposal to make sure that its Full-proof, Legitimate & Reputable! One of the quickest ways to turn a Friend into a Foe & ruin your Reputation is to play with their $ like its "Monopoly-$!" Avoid approaching them with "Get Rich Quick Schemes" or the "You have to Rush & get on board now because it's a Ground-Floor Opportunity." Position yourself so that whenever they hear from you, they* *are eager to hear what you have to offer/say because they believe that you are bringing value or something that can enhance joy, peace & happiness in their life or inner circle.*

* **If you going to hang around "broke-people" make sure that they possess one or more of the following:** *A mind to prosper; A unique talent or skills; Access to Information or contacts.*

*In the guise of Relationships you can be in one of 6-positions: The One; One-Gone, The Next One, The Last One; Not the One & The Only One. Choose Wisely!

*Refuse to drive or operate a vehicle that is not insured except in cases of Extreme Emergency/Life or Death Situations! *It is better to walk, catch a cab or ride with a friend/ neighbor than to operate a vehicle without insurance and have a mishap occur.*

*Never let someone that is irresponsible or incapable of coming up with the insurance deductible drive or operate your vehicle!

Never loan your vehicle to someone non-related unless it's for business purposes or they are working for you in a business capacity!

*Always do visual & functional inspections of a vehicle before you operate it, especially the brakes, tires, fuel & pressure gauges! The Life You Save could be Your Own!

*Always Play by the Rules! Cheaters never prosper! If you don't feel like you can win, then don't get in! You Beat 50% of the people by working hard! You Beat 40% more by doing what's Right! The last 10% is a dogfight! Laws, Rules & Regulations were put in place for a Reason (to maintain order & reduce chaos! If they are to be broken, amended or up-ended please use the proper forum or avenues to bring about a peaceful change.

*If you ever have a legal issue or have to deal with the law; keep your mouth shut and consult with an attorney or a legal-aid society before speaking words that could be used against you in a court

of law! Unspoken words are rarely asked to repeat themselves nor can they be used against you in a court of law.

*Don't Quit Your Day Job until your secondary source and/or side-hustle is bringing in) 3x-4x that of your regular salary. *Sometimes people get caught up on "Hype-Speeches" & "Get-Rich Quick" schemes and forget to wait until the vision manifests before giving up their primary source of income. Use Wisdom! {Sometimes it takes a planted seed 3-5 years to grow into a tree and produce fruit.*

"When GOD gives you a Vision, he will make PROvision!"-George Foster

"When a man gives you a vision, you need to set a deadline of when it will manifest because a goal or a vision without a deadline is just a wish or a dream!"

*When you find an "excuse" don't pick it up!

*Know your strengths and weaknesses. Major in your strengths and manage your weaknesses.

*Specialize in your specialty!

*Eliminate anyone or anything that causes you to be ineffective. *Eliminate anyone or anything that breaks your focus.

*When you show up, a difference should be made!

* Describe how you will solve problems, provide value & reward for your probable purchasers, prospective clients & team members (because you will receive no reward until you do so. $ is a reward you receive when you solve problems for others.

*Don't put Million Dollar ideas into dollar notebooks. Get a leather-bound notebook or a Tablet PC.

*Whenever you see something that makes you smile, buy it and put it in front of you!

*Always check your own parachute and double-check your clip to make sure that you have "real" bullets in it!

*"When things go wrong don't go with them!"-Les Brown

Make your assets pay your liabilities!

Don't expect other people to operate off of the level of knowledge that you have attained!

*Acquire 2-credit cards & build up a limit of at least 2k-10k on each one to have put to the side in case of extreme emergencies or layoffs.

*Get a Universal Life Insurance policy (that has a growth & investment feature where you can pull money out later on) and invest in it on a regular basis {no less than $25 a week. If you ever get sued or worse yet your assets frozen, this will be one of the few items that you own that can't be touched & prove useful in rebounding from some of life's extreme challenges. $25+ a week invested in the right investment vehicle for 20-years would net you over a Million $ anyway.

*Don't let your mate/spouse/significant other leave town or go on a Road-Trip angry at you.

*Design your game plan so that it's

rewarding for those on your team to be in your presence in addition to those who subscribe to your products, goods and services.

* With the game of Life being 90% mental, always approach it with a positive mental attitude and a mindset to dominate, not just participate. When faced with challenging situations, come with the mindset, appearance & approach of a Successful Victory!

*Special Note: Since most people in America are only a paycheck or two away from poverty (even some of those who think that they have risen to affluence), save up the equivalent of 4-paychecks{or more} in your "Emergency-Contingency" fund for those times when life challenges happen & transition periods occur. In addition to this, for those of you who are self-employed, look at investing in a "Roth-IRA" and for those who work for others look at enrolling in your company's 501k program {especially those with company matching} & invest 10% per pay period on a pre-tax basis. In the event *of "lay-offs" or natural disasters you will be glad you did!*

Chapter 26
STAYING MOTIVATED IN THE MIDST OF MAKING CHANGE FOR THE BETTER

Sometimes in the midst of making "**Changes for the Better**"; "*Making Millions*", "*Making Champions*" or "*Major Chess Moves*" there may come moments or times in your life where you may run into or across what is called a "*slump*", a "*Rut*" or a "*Mental Block*" per say or even "*states of depression*" when things get tight or are not going right. It is during times like these when you need to revisit and review your written "*Goals & Aspirations*" in addition to updating your "*Vision Board*" to remind yourself of "**Why**" you are doing this in the first place. Remember that not all things that are worthwhile in Life are not always a "*Sprint*" or an "*Overnight Sensation*" but more so a "*Marathon*" or a "*Journey*". Anything worth having is worth working for. *(Read Proverbs 14:23*

"90% of most Businesses failed because they quit or they had no marketing plan."-Armani Valentino

"80% of your success is going to be achieved by you showing up and being busy."-Armani Valentino

Also remember to work *"Smarter"* in addition to *"Harder"* and keep your eyes on the prize and stay focused. For those times when it may seem that you're lacking in "**Motivation, Inspiration or Encouragement**", you have to find those things that make you happy without causing a hindrance and surround yourself with it or put in front of you.

*"**When you have an Elephant sized Vision, you can't have mosquito faith!**"-Big Ray*

"True Happiness comes from up above and from within"-Big Ray

*Go to Church, get a good workout in, listen to your favorite music that motivates you or go hit a comedy show, concert or play to get your mind moving or flowing. Also look at switching up your diet to more natural energy rich foods, fruits and vegetables. For those times when you need a quick "Pick-me-up" or a sudden change of mindset try a shot of Organic Apple Cider vinegar, Pure/ Tart Cranberry Juice & Reconstituted Lemon Juice to cleanse your body of toxins that may be blocking your creative flow. Sometimes when challenges arise, its best to check and see what's on the inside before you start looking for external causes.

Motivation comes in many shapes, forms and fashions. Whatever it takes to get your "Creative Juices" to flowing "FULL-THROTTLE" , You have to find that "Personal LIKE-Button" and push it as many times as necessary to pump, prime or "Jump-start" your enthusiasm. Whether you're in the midst of "Making Millions" or "Making Champions", some motivational factors may differ while others may remain the same. Below we have listed some *"News that you can use" for intellectual stimulation to change your situation in regards to Mental & Spiritual elevation"*.

-TRIP/ VACATION OR CRUISE

- CHANGE YOUR LOCATION OR OCCUPATION

-SURROUND YOURSELF WITH PEOPLE THAT ARE "ENEMIES OF YOUR WEAKNESSES"

-CHANGE YOUR ATMOSPHERE

-CHANGE YOUR SHOES/ NEW WARDROBE

-TEST DRIVE DREAM CAR OR NEW VEHICLE

-GO TO THE BOOKSTORE AT THE MALL

-LISTEN TO YOUR FAVORITE MUSIC AND/OR UPGRADE YOUR AUDIO SYSYTEM

Special Note: *If your main motivation in Life is obtaining "Material Things" or*

"Monetary" then be mentally prepared for the "Humpty-Dumpty" effect if you don't have balance or a proper "Life" perspective for those times when "Life" challenges do appear or sudden shifts of the market or economy take place.

**Disclaimer: Check with your doctor before you begin any exercise regimen/program, diet or supplemental products! Furthermore, any supplements, exercise regimens, products or services listed in this publication are for example purposes only, not endorsed by the author or publisher and to be used at your own discretion.

Chapter 27
Recommended Readings

*Readers are Leaders! With that being said, we have listed some books below {for informational & reference purposes only} that may help you improve quality of life, work through challenging situations or spearhead/jumpstart creative ideas to come up with solutions to your situations. Stay objective and keep an open mind. Don't always judge a book by its cover or its title. We do not subscribe to nor endorse all concepts or ideas listed in all of the books nor are the opinions contained in them necessarily the opinion of this author.

RECOMMENDED READINGS LIST

50+ AUTHORS & BOOKS THAT YOU MAY WANT TO ADD TO YOUR WEALTH LIBRARY:

"Education is the most Powerful weapon which you could use to change the world."-Nelson Mandela

"90% of most Businesses failed because they quit or they had no marketing plan."-Armani Valentino

"80% of your success is going to be achieved by you showing up and being busy."-Armani Valentino

"You cannot solve a problem from the same consciousness that caused it. You must see the world anew."-Albert Einstein

Some of these Authors & Books will deal with variety and a myriad of topics and subjects that you will encounter as you matriculate in this process called Life. Some will deal with Spirituality, Relationships, Finances, Leadership, Strategy, and The Game of Life in itself to help you to achieve a Balance or Equilibrium if you will and ultimately your Goals in Life. In order to Win in the Game of Life, it would behoove you to know and be aware of various facets and not take a one sided approach so that you can recognize pitfalls and deal with them accordingly or avoid them all together.

In the Sports arena we were taught to not only learn the Offensive, Defensive and Special Teams {or Tactics} side of the Game, but the Business side as well so that one day you can become a "PRODUCER" instead of a "Consumer" or a "Consumable" COMMODITY. There's a Lesson to be learned from everyone {even if it's not to make the same mistakes that they have in the past to avoid bumping your head. We would watch film on ourselves as well as of our opponents on a Regular basis and often times would roll the film back so that we could detect errors, correct mistakes and game plan adequately against the opposition.

There will be times in Life when in order for you to be Successful you will have to develop a competitive advantage which will sometimes include studying the competition or opposition to monitor and notate their tendencies, strategies and mindsets in the guise of game-planning and preparation to achieve optimal results. With that being said, some of the authors on this list may not be a "crowd favorite", but take note: "Favor is not always Fair!" How will you equip yourself for competition or opposition if you don't know or have knowledge of what it is that you're opposing nor whom it is that you're competing against; Sometimes it may be strongholds or principalities. Other times it may a man in an opposite colored uniform or the business across the street.

With knowledge being the new currency, it is better to be on top of your game, instead of the Game being on top of You! The Bible makes reference to "The People shall perish for a lack of knowledge" (Hosea *4:6*). In order to put on the "Full Armor" and fully equip yourself for the task at hand (Ephesians 6:11), its best to be knowledgeable in the arena of which you're competing to eliminate errors and mistakes.

*__*Special Note: R.I.F (READING IS FUNDAMENTAL.__*

__As you pull up and research some of these authors, Remember, "Do not judge a book by its cover or its Title. Most of these authors have more books & literary works than the few that we have listed. Feel free to pursue deeper if you so desire. All of the theories presented in these books and/or manuscripts do not necessarily reflect those of the author of neither this article nor the publisher and are to be referenced for entertainment purposes only. The information contained in these articles & books are not to be construed as Financial nor Medical Advice from the author and if you need guidance or advice to seek the services of a bona fide spiritual leader, a certified financial advisor or a professional health care practitioner .__

*THE BIBLE

*ROBERT T. KIYOSAKI, RICH DAD/ POOR DAD SERIES

*JEFFREY GITOMER, The Little Black Book of Connections & The Little Platinum Book of "Cha-Ching"

*JAY CONRAD LEVINSON
www.GuerillaMarketing.com

*T.D. JAKES, "Before You Do", "Reposition Yourself" & "Maximize The Moment"

*JERRY JONES, Playing to Win

*HANK SEITZ, "Think, Feel & Grow Rich" & "The Happiest Man in the World"

*MIKE MURDOCK, "Enjoy the Winning Life" & "Wisdom for Wining" + Many More! www.WISDOMONLINE.COM

*ARMANI VALENTINO, "Business Warfare" www.ArmaniValentino.com

*SUN TZU

*MARY COLBERT, 13-Women That You Should "NEVER" Marry

*TARIQ NASHEED, The Elite Way

*ROBERT GREENE

*RAY HARDY, "The 7-Figure/ Million Dollar Side Hustle" & "The 48-Laws of Winning"

*WALT FRAZIER, The Game Within The Game

*KAREN RAMSEY, Everything You Know About Money Is WRONG.

*ANDREW LECKEY, The Lack of Money Is the Root of All Evil

*DAVID J. SCHWARTZ, The Magic of Thinking Big

*JALEN ROSE, Got To Give The People What They Want.

*THOMAS J. STANLEY & WILLIAM D. DANKO , "The Millionaire Next Door" & "The Millionaire Mind"

*RAY LINDER, "What Will I Do With My Money"

*C. THOMAS ANDERSON, Becoming a Millionaire God's Way

*GARY V. WHETSTONE, It only Takes One

*KEN IVY, "The Art of Human Chess"

*JERRY R. WILSON, 151-QUICK IDEAS to Get New Customers

*STEPHEN R. COVEY, "The 7-Habits of Highly Effective People"

*RANDALL LANE, P.O.V. LIVING LARGE

*DWIGHT NICHOLS, GOD'S PLANS FOR YOUR FINANCES

*GRANT TEAFF, A COACH'S INFLUENCE/ BEYOND THE GAME

*DON SPEARS

*LEWIS H. WILLIAMS III,
www.iHustleNation.com

*GEORGE S. CLASON, THE RICHEST MAN IN BABYLON

*JOSHUA PIVEN & DAVID BORGENICHT, THE WORST-CASE SCENARIO Survival Handbook

*CRISWELL FREEMAN

*BARBOUR, Armed and Dangerous

*DONALD TRUMP, "The Art of the Comeback" & "How To Get Rich"

*RENNEY MCLEAN, ETERNITY INVADING TIME

*EARVIN "MAGIC" JOHNSON, "32 WAYS TO BE A CHAMPION IN BUSINESS "

*DWIGHT PATE, I THINK I THOUGHT I KNEW!

*DALE CARNEGIE, HOW TO WIN FRIENDS AND INFLUENCE PEOPLE

*BLAINE PARDOE, CUBICAL WAREFARE

*GAME CHANGERS, The World's Leading Entrepreneurs: HOW THEY'RE CHANGING THE GAME & YOU CAN TOO!

*ILYCE R. GLINK, 100 QUESTIONS EVERY FIRST-TIME HOME BUYER SHOULD ASK

*JOHN SPOLESTRA, MARKETING OUTRAGEOUSLY

*ANDREW J. SHERMAN, RAISING CAPITAL

*BRIAN GRAHM, GET HIRED FAST

*JOE GIRARD, MASTERING YOUR WAY TO THE TOP

*NATE ROSENBLATT, ENCYLOPEDIA OF MONEY MAKING $ALES LETTERS

*KEVIN TRUDEAU, "FREE MONEY "THEY DON'T WANT YOU TO KNOW ABOUT" & MANY MORE!

*YOHA LEM, Thinking Out of The Box

*MICHAEL CORBETT, THE 33 RUTHLESS RULES OF LOCAL ADVERTISING

*BARRY CALLEN, PERFECT PHRASES for SALES AND MARKETING COPY

*BOB BEAUDINE, THE POWER OF WHO!

*MICHAEL MACCAMBRIDGE, THE FRANCHISE

*DAN SCHAWBEL, ME 2.0 BUILD A POWERFUL BRAND TO ACHIEVE CAREER SUCCESS

*JOHN JANTSCH, The Referral Engine: Teaching Your Business to Market Itself

*GREG MCKEOWN, ESSENTIALISM

<u>Special Notes:</u> *The less you make, the more you need to study! If you don't have at least 50k minimum in your portfolio, savings or 401k, you don't need to watch TV more than 10-12 hours*

a week. The time used to be entertained can be better utilized to research, enrich or better secure your situation.

"Study to show thyself approved unto God, a workman who needeth not to be ashamed, rightly dividing the word of truth"-2 Timothy 2:15

Chapter 28
Money Making Sales Formulas

*Let me introduce you to a concept and we'll let it marinate for a moment until the lights come on?

> What if you produced a product or a service; an "Instructional DVD"; printed a T-Shirt or wrote a book and sold only 10-items per day in each state with a minimum profit of $5 off of each item or unit sold. Now let's imagine that you're somewhat *"Retired"* and only put in work on an average of 3-8 days a month (around the 1rst, the 3rd & the 15th in the off season and about 8-days or so during the season with guest appearances at events and games included. Now consider what you could bring in with this formula on 3-8 days a month *"work month?"*

For those who aren't good at math or need a "Solution" to this mathematical equation or a few other situations in LIFE, read

"Ecclesiastes 10:19" and then "HIT US UP WHEN YOU'RE READY TO COME UP!"

HOW TO MAKE $1,000,000

- ➢ Sell a $200 product to 5,000 people.
- ➢ Sell a $500 product to 2,000 people
- ➢ Sell a $1,000 product to 1,000 people
- ➢ Sell a $2,000 product to 500 people
- ➢ Sell a $4,000 product to 250 people

- ➢ 5,000 people pay $17/month for 12 months
- ➢ 2,500 people pay $33.50 for 12 months
- ➢ 2,000 people pay $42/month for 12 months
- ➢ 1,000 people pay $84/month for 12 months
- ➢ 500 people pay $187/month for 12 months
- ➢ 250 people pay $335/month for 12 months

*****Special Note:*** *A lot of times when people want to hide something of significance, they hide it in a book. Whatever you want to have in Life or for whatever it is that you want to acquire, they have a book on it. When you sell someone a book, you don't just sell ink & paper, but more so an opportunity for a whole new life if they will just read and apply the knowledge contained within.*

Chapter 29
HUSTLE MODE & *"FLIP-MODE"*

"We are what we repeatedly do. Excellence therefore is not an act, but a HABIT!" – Aristotle

"80% of your success is going to be achieved by you showing up and being busy." –Armani Valentino

"90% or most businesses failed because they quit or they don't have a Marketing Plan." – Armani Valentino

"People do not decide to become extraordinary. They decide to accomplish extraordinary things." –Edmund Hillary

The first thing you need to do before you go into *"Hustle Mode or Flip Mode"* is to make a decision to just that and devise a plan. Once you have a plan in hand, put your *"Game-*

face" on, "**Adjust your Attitude**" and "**Get Your Mind Right**" because it's "**GAME-TIME**"! Not only do you need to have a "**Positive Mental Attitude**"; you need to have a "**Go Get it Attitude.**"

"When you go out to compete, you have to compete like you are running in the Kentucky derby!"-Bishop Don "Magic" Juan

HUSTLE-MODE

Sometimes in the guise of "**getting your hustle on**" or increasing your infrastructure to get a "**bigger piece of the pie**", you have to transform your mindset to encompass the tasks at hand or associated with creating a financial empire or portfolio. Similar to that of a "Prime Athlete" as he prepares to compete, you have to put your "game-face" on and have your mind, body and soul conditioned to go "a full 4-Quarters" and several overtimes if necessary in order to fulfill or achieve your goals. You have to be "Relentless" like a boxer in a Prize fight where the only way you lose is if you quit fighting or allow your opponents to outwork you and get knocked out. Once you step in to your arena or area of expertise, you need to be focused and **check all *"distractions"* and *"unnecessary baggage"* or *"dead-weight"* prior to leaving the house or in the parking lot; because 1-mistake could cost you your opportunity or set you back to ground zero.**

"The Quickest Way to get defeated is to Lose Focus."

Whatever your venture, product or service, your job is to make it *"Grow, Go & Get some More!"* With Prior Preparation Preventing Poor Performance, you need to be at least 3-steps ahead of the game and be prepared to adapt and adjust to certain shifts or changes in momentum during those times when Life throws you a curve to still obtain optimal results and give yourself a cushion to absorb or deflect any unforeseen blows, hits or accidents. There will be times in Life where you may not achieve every goal within the allotted period of time or reach the finish line before every competitor. Sometimes, you don't always win by crossing the finish line first, but more so by crossing the finish line. This is what may be referred to as a *"Pass/Fail"* option which is determined solely on the participation and productivity of the participant. It's not always how you start, but how you finish. When you start an assignment, task or enter into a competition, competed and complete the assignment or task as if you were working for **GOD,** your family or a special cause and *"losing is not an option."* Prepare your mind, body and soul to complete your task regardless of circumstances and not get weary in well doing. If you are in business, finish what you start and get a polished/ finished product to the people and communicate with your client base in the event of temporary setbacks. If you're competing in the sports arena, always compete and perform to the best of your ability as to win the prize regardless of the activity of those around you or lackluster performances by teammates. If your arena is entertainment, the show must go on and *"1-monkey doesn't stop the show."* If you are an entrepreneur, have a product, service or manufacturing don't give up or quit in the face of adversity, because you'll win if you don't quit.   When situations arise and it appears that you may have to call a proverbial *"time-out"*, complete and fulfill all current/present orders and put future orders on hold unless fulfilling current orders would present a health risk.

When you experience a nice payday, *"hit a lick"* or have a successful venture, don't go and blow all of the profits. Restock, *"Re-up"* or reinvest a certain percentage of the profits back into the business to make sure that you have operating capital and materials to function in the future during tight turbulent times or when things get slow in the financial arena or due to seasonal demands. If your business or venture deals with non-perishable goods, get about 3-weeks -3- months of goods and supplies stocked up in advance. If your business or venture deals with perishable goods, then you should have at least 3-days of advance stock on hand in addition to 5-10 additional supplier resources in case your primary source dries up or experiences adversity and is unable to deliver. Just because 1 source or entity stops producing, doesn't mean that you have to stop producing.

"FLIP-MODE"

"Flip-Mode" is when you get into a mindset of "***Go get it***" or "***Get it done Now and in a Hurry***", sort of like cutting Light switches *"On or Off"* to achieve a goal at a rapid pace or in a short period of time.

A Business Model example of *"Flip-Mode"* is trying to move a mass or a quantity of a product or service in a short amount of time to reach Fiscal, Financial or corporate goals. Another example can be the attempt to move a mass or quantity amount of *"product/service -A"* or *"product/service -A"* as a whole in order to acquire *"product/service -B"* or *"item-C"* in the guise of expansion, upgrading or fulfilling a Need, Want or Desire.

Other Times, *"Flip-Mode"* can be in the guise of fund-raising where as you will acquire a mass or quantity of *"product/service -A"* at a wholesale or reduced rate and resell it at a rate above wholesale and sometimes below retail to make acquisition of the product in a short period of time more attractive & conducive to mass purchases and self-promotion (commonly known as *"The Hook-Up"* in common vernacular.

Whenever you get into *"Flip-Mode"*, it is very important that you don't let your ego or attitude or enthusiasm override *"common-sense"* {which isn't so common anymore) or good judgment.

"Never make a Long-Term Decision based upon a Short-Term Situation."

Before you enter into a venture to acquire and resale products or services that are not already in your repertoire or inventory, first make sure that it is Legal, Ethical & Practical. Don't just go for a *"Song & a dance"* or sales pitch by some slick salesman. Do your own research to make sure that its reasonable and feasible in addition to taking a survey to make sure that there is a market and a demand for these products /services and that a demand can be supplied in a sufficient amount of time once a demand is created. Do not get caught up in the *"Hype"* of "*You have to get in now on the Ground floor of this opportunity."*   If the product/service is that Great, they will either remanufacture or reproduce more when supplies get low or it will create a need for a substitute good which might end up being your new niche.

"Necessity is the mother of Invention."

When you go into *"Flip-Mode"* with your own products & services, make sure that you get focused on the task at hand and be cognizant of the various differences of markets and the customer base that you will be serving, in addition to making sure that you are organized before you leave the House. Same thing goes for your team if you have one.

"3-Things will get you beat in this "Game", Being Un-Organized, Un-Disciplined & Un-Conditioned!"

"The Quickest Way to get defeated is to Lose Focus."

Other Factors that will contribute to your Success in *"Flip-Mode"* are:

- Your Mood & Attitude as well as your approach.
- Food, Nutrition and Proper Rest prior to event
- Exercise, Fitness Level and proper Conditioning.
- A fertile market or environment with qualified prospects that have a willingness and ability to purchase or subscribe to your products, goods or services.
- Prior Preparation and Proper Promotion.

- Appearance, Attire, Grooming and Mode of Transportation, because sometimes it's not always about getting from Point "A" to Point-"B", but more so of how you arrive.
- Whether or not your Product /Service helps to Make $, Save $, Time, Energy or Efforts.

****Special Note:** Attitude, Approach and Location play a very important part in your success when going into "Flip-Mode". The same effort that it takes to make "dimes or a few dollars" in one market can be utilized to make "Millions" in another market that's ripe, fertile and receptive to your products/ services, concepts or ideas. With the "Right Research" & Prior Preparation, you can come up "Exponentially" in a market that's "starving" or "thirsty" for your concepts & ideas. By utilizing the concepts of the Laws & Rules of "Supply & Demand" in a proper fashion, your product/services can become a "Household" name. A prime example of this is one of my good friends that was famous in the clothing industry who* *used to make $2k-5k daily and $7k-12k a day on the weekends vending & selling T-shirts, hats & concession items after an NBA-Team won "Back-to-Back" Championships. Way back in the day, when the author was new to the game and in college, I tapped into this concept (with only $60 in my pocket) and made $2,300*

{actually it was more like $2,700 but I had spent $400 on Entertainment, Travel & Expenses + Restocking} in an 18-hour period working for someone else on a road trip making only $2-5 commission per item. Imagine what had happened when I had branched out and went independent? Now you see why the college days are supposed to be some of the Best days of your Life. My theory is that it doesn't have to stop there, (because Life is an ever learning experience) if you continue the concepts and continually discover new markets and territories. New Champions are being made in various entities and markets Year Round. All you have to do

is tap into the "Source" & "Supply a Need".

Chapter 30
The Acknowledgements Chapter:
aka-"*The Treasure Chapter*"

The Acknowledgements Chapter: aka "The Treasure Chapter"

+With Success in Life being a Team-Effort, I would like to say that I didn't get here by myself and would like to give credit where credit is due. First and foremost I thank GOD for his son JESUS, his Word and for protecting (from the seen & un-seen) & providing for me! Without him, I am nothing. I am giving GOD The Glory for choosing & giving me the strength, wisdom, guidance, knowledge and the experiences to write this book. (Mathew 22:14, Proverbs 14:23 & Mathew 6:21)

"To them that much is given, much is required." In my never ending quest for Success and my relentless pursuit of Excellence (even against insurmountable odds) I can sometimes seem demanding as well as insensitive to mediocrity,

complacency & incompetence. For those on my team as well as those that I have encountered along this journey called life (even some of the haters because everybody plays an important part in the ecosystem) I always wanted the Best for US and have nothing but Love for YOU! {When you Love somebody or something, you will go above & beyond to make sure that they are successful or to help them to survive.} **"Everybody Loves a Winner"** *(except for the one that just lost, got cut or traded before the playoffs!) If you don't see your name listed in this section don't be upset, just be more productive & proactive in your life as well as mine. (Get with me on the side & we'll see if we can get you listed in the next book, plenty more to come. We had to get this one out to the printer before the year end!)*

+In our philosophy of empowering & sharing the wealth with those who helped us to acquire it, we are promoting & giving back to some of those who have helped us along this journey called Life. If you see yourself listed consider yourself blessed as well as a Blessing. Highlight yourself and show it to your friends & family then tell 10-people to buy a book. If you see someone listed that has a business and you are in need of their services or in their town, stop by and talk to them Quick! You'll be Surprised at what you might Get! (Don't forget to spend some $ with them and ask for "The Big-Ray $pecial" or to mention that you were referred by Chosen One Sports.)

Imagine the Economic Impact that could be made if just 300 of you would spend just a mere $10-20 a month with each of the following entities/businesses listed in this chapter on essential services or products that you were going to utilize or acquire anyway + save $ and get more bang for your "buck" ? Sometimes in the guise of making $ or saving $(which both make sense) you have to give {sowing $} in order to Receive. If you took a look at the average cost of acquiring a new customer/client which averages between $28-$42 each on the low end & up to $128-$242+ to attract higher end clientele you come out much better spending some $ with someone that can return the favor and not get taxed like you're a resident of 2-countries.

I would like to give thanks to my family {Parents, siblings, Grand Parents(RIP), Aunts, Uncles, Nephews, Nieces, Cousins & extended families) starting with one of the Greatest Life Coaches & Financial Planners of my time, my Father Ronald Hardy who also happens to have 2-Collegiate & 2-State Championships under his belt.

I would also like to thank my Beautiful Mother Dorothy Hardy who was a Campus Queen and a Champion at Academic Games who taught me the importance of showing up for work or practice on time or before time!

*I would like to acknowledge my Great Brother Ram (Ram-Jam Sports & Entertainment who started winning at a young age and now as an adult is instrumental in helping several well known Actors, Entertainers, Boxers & World Champion Athletes reach their pinnacle and peak in their careers as a result of his association with them in addition to his affiliation with several NBA Championship teams in addition to Coaching & mentoring youth in High School and on the AAU teams that he sponsors to go to National Tournaments & Championships every year.

*Special Credit goes out to my Great Sister Rhonda who is in my estimation "**one of The Greatest Sisters that ever walked the planet**". We would like to thank her for her countless hours of consultation that her firm has donated and invested into this project as well as what they have sowed into my life. Speaking of Credit, she can help you to clean your credit up in 3-6 months and have you "rolling right" & *"smelling like a rose" Thanks for the hook-up on the S-Class. The Mansion is coming next.*

*Special Shout-Out to my Nephew of the Year Kharon (www.AppleTradeUSA & www.ElectronicTradeUSA.com) for keeping me up to date on the latest communication & electronic devices and for hooking me and my players up on how to get the High-end luxury autos at "The Players Price"! *We started him out early in life on these concepts and he came up nicely! He used to make $150-250 daily selling candy in Middle School & High School and had 2 cars by the* *age of 14 + the money to get someone to chauffeur him around until he got a license. He parlayed these funds and invested in a landscaping/snow removal company with 5 employees in addition to a mobile detailing business with the pressure washer built inside of the truck of which he sold the business for $25k after his 2nd year of college to concentrate more on his studies. He is also known as a talented web developer who can put your message in the atmosphere with no fear.*

*For those that like sports keep an eye out for my MVP-nephew Amauri (www.AmauriMVP.com) who has amazed Basketball fans nationwide since he was a toddler! Now highly ranked as one of the top Basketball players in the country he's being recruited & scouted by most major programs (as well as the PROS) and up for the Mr. Basketball award 2017'.
http://rayforddevteam.neocities.org/

*Special Recognition goes out to my gorgeous niece Kiara aka *"Pretty Baby Ki-ki"* with Rayford Investments in Miami who has been applying a lot of the concepts listed in this book. (She is also the owner of "Ki-ki La-LA" Salon & Immaculate Cleaning Services of Detroit with over 35 employees). *Not bad for someone who was making 6-figures before the age of 22!* {Now her new nickname is *"Money-making Pretty Baby Ki-ki"*!

Although there are many who have contributed to my success (to many to notate or mention) I would like to give special thanks to some who have had concentrated efforts in helping me in my ascension towards greatness, because I didn't get here by myself.

---

*The Hardy Family, The Jones Family, The Benifield Family, The Sharpe Family & all the rest of my family world-wide!

*The Wong Family (Faith-Image Consultant @ The Faith Touch-B.R., La & LA, Ca, Cy & Betty-RIP) www.TheFAITHTouch.com

*The Hill family(Winston, Fannie, Chip, Wendell & Whitney), *The Suber Family especially Dorothy Suber-RIP who taught me the importance of having a Product & a Service at a young age. *The Calloway Family;

*The Hamlin Family (Angie @ Hamlin BBQ & Strictly Sportswear Who inspired me to "Up my Game" & move a volume of products to make more in addition to dress to be the Best! Kathy @ Strictly Sportswear-Detroit, Mi who is a Legend in the Game and has been outfitting "Players, Ballers, Athletes & Entertainers for Decades; & Dr. Calvin Hamlin who can show you how to make sense out of nonsense;

*The Ballards,

*The Carnes Family (The Best Neighbors we ever had!

*Victor "Vic" Adams **One of the Greatest Talent Scouts Ever**! I patterned part of my game from observing him as I grew up. Whenever I needed a new school/college to attend, he always had one waiting in the wings! He and his boy **Noel Brown** are partially responsible for me completing my College education and I am forever Grateful.

*The Horatio William Foundation (It's always good to have a philanthropist on your team! www.HoratioWilliamsFoundation.org

*Rev. Tyrone Hannah & Family + Cornerstone Christian Fellowship-The Colony, TX,

*Pastor Ralph N. Moore (Victory & Power Ministries-B.R, La. & WPFC-Radio. www.DrRalphMoore.com & www.wpfc1550am.com) This man taught us the importance of Victorious living and strongly emphasized the principles of: Accountability, Responsibility & Discipline. He encouraged entrepreneurship and for everybody in the congregation to support one another's businesses. Check out his books on his website.

*Bishop T.D. Jakes (The Potter's House-Dallas, TX www.ThePottersHouse.org) Check out his books including "Reposition Yourself", "Before You Do" & "Maximize the Moment."

*Pastors Joseph & Dr. Bridgette Steib- The Ministry of Love-B.R., La. www.MinistryOfLove.com

*Coach Earnest Thomas-RIP(Who taught us the power of Thinking Big & Visualizing Success!

*Coach James Anderson, Thanks for helping me and a lot of my players with our financial aid. Due to your assistance, mentoring & coaching, college was definitely some of the Best Days of our Lives!

*Scott Bradford aka "Big-Scott"-RIP (A TRUE CHAMPION

*Cousin Harry Jones with "Harry's Ribs & Chicken"- Detroit(MI.

*The Mackey Family ,Robert, Jackie & Roderick;

*The Higgins Family-Brian, Regina & BJ;

*Everetta Edwards -If you need marketing/publicity for your product, service or events, their company can pump you up like the "Old-school Reeboks" www.KustomEvents.com . If you're in need of a "Press-Conference" or "Draft-Day" Suit,

get at her for custom tailored looks at the Team Rate or Player's Price! Check out Everlux Custom Clothiers: www.EverLux.net D.C., Miami. If your order is substantial, they can even fly in & size you up with a deposit;

*Keegan McIntosh, Les Brown, Kevin Lloyd, Mike Hill, Ken Davis,

*The Lake Highlands Wildcats Youth Association (www.LHWYA.COM) { Coach Mackey & Mrs. Mackey, Coach Mike Nixon, Coach Dre'- Andre Young, Coach Hall "Everybody Loves a Winner", Coach Derrick Tyler & The Wildcats Fans & Family who helped us to Win Those Bowl-Games, Championships & Tournaments.

*Andy Brown (Author & Radio Personality www.AndyBrownSpeaks.com ; www.TheOnlineHappyHour.com & www.iLifeRadio.com

*Kevin Hopwood & J.R. (The Mastermind behind "TMi-Media Group" www.TMiRadio.com "Global, National & Local". When you have music or a message that you need to go around the world, this is

one of the places that you want to utilize to get it there.

*Dewayne Bryant -owner of the Ten-11 Grill- Dallas, TX www.TenElevenGrill.com ,

*Robert Pierce (www.CarnivoXO.com),

*The Mims Family, Brothers Garnett, www.MusclesInMotionSystems.com ; www.LinemenOnly.com ; Publicist David aka "Daveed" with Det2LA.com & the marketing firm of Mims & Nem "Making It Mean Something"; + their nephew Jamone;

*REGINALD GRANT, MSEd. The founder of the Grant Language Academy, this guy is multi-faceted & multi-talented & He wears many hats such as a Professor, Instructor, Coach, Author, Entrepreneur, and Philanthropist. He is a noted Speaker on the Lecture circuit who is well connected & respected Nationwide who was instrumental in me getting some of my manuscripts out. Check out his new book 'Success Stories Insights by African American Men" and look him up online.

www.ReginaldGrant.com
www.AFamilyOfAuthors.com

www.GrantLanguageAcademy.com
www.eSportsInstruction.com

*Joan Louis- An innovator and a Trend-setter in the Hair Industry who showed me how to tap into a Billion dollar industry & come out with an adequate piece of the pie. Owner of MoHair Salon-Baton Rouge, La. www.MoHairOnline.com

*Michael Towns
(www.WhoIsMichaelTowns.com) & The Twins (You know who you are!)

*"Rocki" Raquel Sawyer, President of Detroiters in Dallas. It's amazing how you put this thing together & keeps it running smoothly with so many complex & diverse personalities;

Nathaniel "Gooney" Hampton, Bridget Small, Big-Duke, Charles Hearns,

* Adrian Harris, Thanks for helping the vision to manifest!

*Adrian Miller & Family-Owner of Sweet-Sweet-backs Bad Azz Bones & Dirty Mac's BBQ-Ft. Worth, TX; He has that flavor that you savor & that "killer-sauce!"

*Robert Williamson & his sister Sandra;

*Pastor Freddie Haynes- Friendship West Baptist Church-Dallas, Texas www.friendshipwest.org

*Ocie Taylor with Taylor's Floors in Ft. Worth, TX. He puts it down with Precision! Quality Work at a Reasonable Price! www.TaylorFlooringTx.com)

*Terry Sullivan (www.AllAmericanBowl.com),

*Amber Davies-A female that's making an impact in a man's game with the NFL-Houston Texans Scouting Dept. www.HoustonTexans.com ,

*Armani Valentino- Author/Motivational Speaker & owner of College Boy Publishing www.ArmaniValentino.com,

Arnold Nevels, Arnold "Darnel" Woods, Howard Fanning, Steve Harvey, Bernie Mac- RIP;

* Angela Williams- The owner of Dorroyz Hair Loss Solutions in Arlington, TX has helped men, women & children with hair loss issues grow healthy hair using non-surgical methods.

www.DorroyzHairLossSolutions.com

* Comedian Anastasia "The Bold" Bolden' (she's one of the top female comedians in the DFW-Metroplex that will definitely get an audience's attention.
www.AnastasiaTheBold.com

*Shemeika Wright -Wrightway Tax Services- Dallas, Texas. *"Where you can get your taxes done the Wright-way"*
www.wrightwaytaxservices.net

*Coach Andy Hispher, Coach Damon Stodimire (He was also "Cold-Blooded as a Player'! Coach Mike Barrow, Coach Doug Smiley,

*My boy "Big-Charles" (Charles Wynn the gospel percussionist;

*Dimetria Wright -Wright Legal Services - B.R., La. They can help you to go from *"Hot Water"* to a fresh cup of tea for a small fee!

*Coach Eric Jones (aka "Big-E"; who is one of the most prolific and inspirational Coaches & D-Line trainers in Texas. He stresses the importance of *"Putting yourself in position to Win!"*

*Coach Brad Frazier

(www.OldSchoolQuarterbacks.com),

*Coach Blake Frazier-CFL-Scout for the Roughriders & JC-Coaching Legend who is One of the 2 football guru's that I consult when going up against a formidable opponent to set game plans to shut them down like K-mart or dissect them like a frog in Biology class.),

*Coach Wilfred Thomas who helped me to set an indoor scoring Record in the All American Bowl in addition to instilling in me a phrase that I utilize in my daily walk; "Yeah though I walk through the Valley of The Shadow of Death, I will fear no Evil. WHY? BECAUSE I'M THE BADDEST CAT IN THE JUNGLE!"

*Coach Rodney Blackshear, Former Texas Tech great and AFL-Iron-man, now One of the Great Offensive Minds in the game of Football. He has taken arena routes & applied them to the 11-man game with astounding results,

*Coach Curtis Blackwell (One of the top College Recruiting Coordinators & developers

of talent in the country with Sound Mind/Sound Body Football Camps which attracts the Top Football Players & College Coaches from all over America. www.SMSBcamp.com

*Coach Les Miles-I appreciate you for coming in to present me with the Nike Coach of the Year Award www.LesMiles.com ,

*Coach Frank Wilson- In every major program there is a coach behind the scenes that helps to make things go Great & he is one of them! Now that his hard work has paid off, he has been catapulted into the forefront as a leader of his own program and took them to a Major Bowl Game his first year.

*Coach Nick Saban- All he does is WIN, wherever he goes! He also has one of the most intense Football Camps in the Country.

*Coach Bobby Wilson is another coach behind the scenes who helps to propel his program to National Championships,

*Coach Gary Patterson- an intense coach with a passion for perfection & one of the few to ever have a perfect season 12-0;

*Mike Sinqfield, (Director of Football Operations at TCU

*Coach Tommie Robinson-Wherever he goes, College or PRO he is producing Results & coming out on Top.

*Coach Will Martin- Check out his DVD for DB's on www.CoachesChoice.com,

*Cedric Fails- Accountant and Owner of C.G. Fails & Associates Accounting Firm-Detroit, Mi. where they keep your books tight & your money Right! www.CGFails.com ;

*Gerald Wade, Financial Analyst with the Coca-Cola bottling company of Atlanta.

*Derrick Vaughn aka "DJ-Chill" www.IamBossmanDino.com

*Coach Christian Vitale (www.TheKickIsUp.com)

*Maurice Stokes-aka Mo-Tickets & Mo-Cars-Dallas, TX;

*Roy Tarpley,-RIP (former schoolmate & NBA 6th man of the year;

*Tim Autry-The Ultimate Realtor, Tina Cooper-Tyler & Family;

*Todd Cadwallader (Premier Youth Football League www.PYFL.com),

 Ms.Dorris, Pacific Island Athletic Association;

*Hassan Barzani (One of the Best Interns that we've ever had! It's time to make that money! You need your own Product Line!

*Barbara Thompson, Joy Stephens, www.kidswellcare.com; www.t30andbeyond.com , Coach Willie Tyson,

*Nicole Johnson (Owner-Hands of Glory Salon-Dallas,   TX www.HandsOfGlorySalon.net),

*Gene Thrash - The owner of Corganics Inc. He has a Great Product called "RELIEF" and it really works! One of his associates had approached us about marketing/promotions for the company & gave us some samples. A few days later I incurred a freak accident getting out of the shower and ended up having a knee injury. Long story short, I ended up using the product and am now a customer as well! www.Corganics.com

*Bret Cooper (The Director of the Junior Academic All-American Bowl & the High School All-American game who creates opportunities for youth nationwide. Well Connected, Well Respected. Often Imitated, never duplicated, he has set the bar in Youth Sports & All-Star Games. www.BretCooperFootball.com)

*Marshal Fortson(5-LINX), Steve Carter(5-LINX), Lee Lemons(5-LINX),Catherine Harvey(5-LINX),Reginald Edwards(5-LINX),Rosa Battle(5-LINX),Thomas McLemore(NFL-Detroit & Indianapolis, Jimmy Johnson(NFL, *Chris Scott Sr.& Jr.,

*William Kareem Baker-One of the up & coming Sports video filming editors with "Phenom World Sports",

*Tony Stephens(Primerica), Urshula Udics, Coach Hugo Hughes,

*Kevin Burrell & Family,

*Cheron K. Griffin, Author & host Reality TV show "Preachers Ex'es" www.CheronKGriffin.com),

*Pastor Renney McClean & Family-Check out his book "Eternity Evading Time", www.RMMinistries.com

*Pastor Bill Earley,

*Pastor Gene Peyton,

*Dr. Mike Murdock-Ft. Worth, TX. His books; DVD's & Lectures have not only inspired me to reach additional levels of Greatness and overcome obstacles, but has helped a lot of my Players & Coaches as well. I usually take a couple of his books with me when I travel, especially to the Big Games & I always happen to bump into him at the airport as he travels spreading the Good News of JESUS CHRIST and helping people to break the back of poverty. His messages impart so much knowledge & wisdom that they can elevate your Spirit, your mind and your bank account if you let it. www.WisdomCenter.cc

*The Late Gerald Levert-RIP; The Late Emanuel Steward-RIP; Brian McKnight; Kem, Damien Butler-Owner of The North Texas Express & Sports agent.

*Caesar -with www.DALLASGospelConnection.com & The Pipkin Law firm has helped several of my clients come up like the Jefferson's & live like Jed Clampet in the Beverly Hillbilly's!

*Denise Joyner (www.exclusif-e.com)

*Mary Pierce & her son Donte (www.UrHappyHouse.com)

*Rev. Henry Parker-Ark. Bapt. Univ. Evangelist Yundrae Wilson, Suebe Herring,

*Michael McDonald aka "Big-Mike"-European Basketball Player & Event Promoter–Dallas, TX. www.BigMikeEvents.com

*Luther Coppage- A Master Strategist & VP of www.LucysLingerie.com based in Beverly Hills, Ca & Las Vegas, NV who showed me how to stay abreast of not only current, but future trends to stay ahead of the game & come out sweet smelling.

*Craig Spruill with Playmaker Sports Marketing www.PLYMKRSSPRTS.COM

*Dr. Elizabeth Branch has an excellent concept for helping students and athletes to improve their grades & test scores. Check out www.CollegeBoundBallerz.org

*Dr. Theodore B. Riley aka "Big-Ted"; Carolyn Miller aka "Cee Millions" with N Control Records; Robin Robinson;

*Lori Rambo aka Comedian "Sommore", She is one of the Original Queens of Comedy & considered one of America's top female entertainers; she has mystified fans & sold out venues nationwide. www.Sommore.com

*D. Elli$-Dallas King of Comedy aka Mr. Entertainment! The comedian-actor-musician is a "Triple-Threat" in the entertainment field and will have you coughing up a lung laughing. www.dEllisWorld.com

*Lavelle Crump aka "David Banner" (Former schoolmate & SGA/ Student Body President turned Rapper, Actor & Music producer & Civil Rights Activist who literally carries the state of Mississippi on his back.

*Carlton Mosley aka "Cool-C" who set the Hair-World on fire and gave them chills at the same time with his ICE-Magazine & Product

line, Beauty School & performances in Hair-Battles around the country. His hairstyles set world-wide trends of which many renowned hair-stylists patterned their game after. In high-demand as a host, speaker & instructor he set the bar in the Urban hair industry.

*Myra Brazile, "Bad-Boy"-Jermaine-Det. Mark Macon(NBA),

*Maurice Smith @ Encore Salon-Southfield, Mi,

*Romel Russell aka Martez owner of Paparazzi & Imaginations Salons in B.R., La,

*George Hunt- The Owner of *"Tight-Fades"* Barbershop in B.R, La.

*DJ 4.0 (www.fourpointohh.com).

*DJ Gary Chandler (the World Renown Turntable Technician at Hot 107.5 in Detroit who is still putting it down for the Crown. Early in my career, he and a few other DJ's were instrumental in drawing large crowds of epic proportions to my events that funded a portion of my college experience. This guy single handedly made a Restaurant Franchise

the top selling unit in America with his music and it's still #1 for over a decade thanks to him. If you want to make your music famous, pack a venue or supply the sounds that can stimulate your bank account, check out www.DJGARYCHANDLER.COM

*Special Shout-out to my boy Wan Ali originally from Chicago with Wan-Wear –Las Vegas, NV who custom makes our hats & apparel for major events & special occasions. Check him out (www.WanWear.com & www.WanAli.com) .We were down from day-1 since we met at the Superbowl in 98' and now he is a household name among the nation's elite athletes & entertainers. With "A-List" clients such as Presidents, Senators, Mega-Superstars & more, if you need your campaign or wardrobe to be "Outstanding", he is the man with an outstanding wardrobe plan!

*Vincent Viott Mann-The other football guru that I consult when going up against a formidable opponent for Un-stoppable

Offensive schemes that will allow me to open up the Offense like Wal-Mart franchises & Put points on the board like a Las Vegas slot machine. On Defense he is one of the originators who helped me to develop my own versions of "The Gangster" & "The Worlds-Greatest" Defenses that are designed to stop people in their tracks like glue style 'Rat-Traps!" His Special Teams play mystifies opponents & keeps the fans on their seats. "Don't look behind you, because he might be in front of you!" Don't let the smooth taste fool you!

*Clarence Larry Jackson & Family-Owner of CJ's Barber & Beauty Salon-B.R., La.

*Eric Fowler (E's Tee's); The Late Michael "Bear" Taliaferro-RIP; The Late Lyle Alzado-RIP; Gregory Wade,

*The Late Al Davis-RIP, Owner of the Oakland Raiders." Just Win Baby", He is still winning long after he's gone),

*Wyatt Harris- Director of www.SonicBoomTraining.com A former teammate whose work ethic was

unparalleled. He emphasized the importance of utilizing martial arts techniques to give you an advantage over your opponents in sports and in life.

*Darren Deloatche- A No-Nonsense Sports Agent & Scout who gets you more "Bang for the Buck" www.AscensionEntInc.com

*Attorney Sadat Montgomery- If you ever get "*Hit*" in an accident; call or hit up Sadat at (214)DESERVE and get what you deserve! www.214Deserve.com Dallas, TX. I like the way he has his phone # built in his web address! I wonder where did he got that idea from?

*Atty. Dr. Harry Washington Ezim-B.R, La.

*Atty. Elvin Sterling-B.R., La. -Not only was he tenacious on the field as a football player & Student Government President in college, He is tenacious in the courtroom as well. Also owner of Sterling construction where they can put it together in any kind of weather.

*Germaine 'Germany" Miller with Joasie Mae's Restaurant & Aunt-G's Pies in LA, Ca. & N.O., La)

*Kenneth Grover
www.UndergroundRecruit.wordpress.com,

*Mike Fenske & Steve Lickman (with MJF Football Recruiting
www.MJFFootballRecruiting.com),

*Brodrick Sublet- This Former Arena Football Player & now Coach is also one of the Top HS Recruiting Coordinators in Dallas, TX is truly an asset to every program that he embraces.

*Ryan Johnson-One of the Top Promoters as well as one of the Top Male Hair Stylists in Dallas, TX. www.Studio5012.com

*Fred Banks- aka "Casino"-Promoter & CEO of World Wide Entertainment Group and *Owi-Events* based out of Dallas, TX who produces & promotes *"mind-boggling"* events. www.VIPofDallas.com   & www.TruthNightClubDallas.com

*Chris Butler - The CEO of ICON-Entertainment Group. When you need an event developed, marketed or promoted, he's the man with the plan.

*Andre Lang aka *"Ft. Worth Dre"* -Promoter & Graphic Artist-Fort Worth, Texas.

*Gregland Burns aka *"DeVille"* The Legendary Promoter and Creative Director of one of the most innovative Event marketing tools in Texas. Not only can he fill large auditoriums with a single "E-blast", he can make you or your event *"FAMOUS"* and an overnight sensation. www.PartyChaser.com

*Rume w/Devin the Dude (Singer, Song-writer, Actor, Musician extraordinaire who has been putting in work on tours across America. http://www.RumeWorld.com

*Solomon Page-Former NFL-Player with the Cowboys/Chargers and Founder of Step Into Excellence Motivational Speaking & Training.

*Todd Krueger-Elite QB Trainer & Coach www.PlayQB.com

*Yusef Chew, Coach Farasi Norman, Glen "Big-Baby" Davis (NBA; Antoine Joubert, Shaquille O'Neal, Shannon Murphy with The Making of Champions who gave me a whole new insight on Special Teams Play, Coach Maurice Burris, Coach Milton Wallace,

*Monja Qui with www.QuiEntertainment.com

*Coach Torlonzo Tate
www.LouisianaEagles.com

*Coach Marino Casem (We don't reward losing), Coach Haynes (Kenner Chiefs & the N.Orleans Knights; Dr. Amber Banks, Roosevelt Johnson,

*Sydnee Turner –She has a passion for graphics like we have a passion for sports! (www.SydGrafix.com),

*Selwyn Harris & Pedro over at www.VolvoOfDallas.com for the many miracles that they have worked to get people rolling for little or nothing down.

*Tammie Riggs-Former Bank Executive, Grant Writer & VP, now turned philanthropist who puts Student Athletes in touch with a good dose of *"Reality"* when it comes to

Recruiting.
www.StudentAthletesInTouch.com),

*Tamara Goodwin {Actress & Model that gets the job done in good taste. www.TamaraGoodwin.com ;

*Larry Brown-NFL 94'Superbowl MVP www.MetroplexSelect.com & www.ColleyvilleCowboys.com

*Mike "Scooter" McGruder, NFL-49'ers/Patriots. Showed me how not to get fooled by elaborate passing schemes.

*Byron Williams-President of the NFL-Players Association-Dallas Chapter & member of the 87' Superbowl Champs-NY-Giants who caught the Winning Touchdown. www.FootballMiniCamps.com Also hit him up if you need a stadium built or Tire Turf installed.

*Spud Webb- former NBA-Dunk Champion & Current GM of The Texas Legends-NBA-D-League www.TexLegends.com

*Myles White-One of the Top-3 WR's to ever come through Chosen One Sports.(NFL-Green Bay Packers/NY Giants & Jets who

started 7 games as a Rookie the year after the Packers last Super Bowl victory.

*Lomas Brown, NFL-HOF Detroit Lions

*Aeneas Williams (NFL-HOF. One of my former team mates who is a testament that submitting to the Will of GOD and the authority of CHRIST along with hard work pays off. James 4:10 & Proverbs 14:23. He is an Achiever! He set goals and he accomplished them against insurmountable odds. Pick up a copy of his book "IT TAKES RESPECT". Also if you are ever in Phoenix or St. Louis stop by one of his churches and take in a worship service.

*Maurice Hurst (NFL-Patriots. Another one of my ex-Team mates who overcame insurmountable odds to make it and last 9 years on one of the toughest teams in the NFL. Currently working as an NFL Scout.

*Donald Fusilier- one of the Top-3 WR's to come through Chosen One Sports who overcame adverse obstacles in life and still persevered to produce optimal Results! A true student & now a Master of the Game who is a testament that "Hard work pays off, when channeled in the proper direction. Google search or look up on YouTube.com *"The Donald Fusilier Horror Show".* You will be AMAZED as he "Lights the Fuse"! Check out his book "The Donald Fusilier story"

*Thomas "Pepper" Johnson-former High School & College All-American@ Ohio St. /All-PRO NFL-LB(Giants, Jets, Lions, Patriots/Future HOF & Super-bowl Champion turned Coach who "Hit-Hard" every play! He taught me the important lesson early in my career to be careful of whom you let in your inner circle & that you can't hang out with everybody.

*Quentin McKinney- *"The Dallas Legend"* is **The Best WR to never go PRO!** He is the equivalent of Basketball's Earl "The Goat" Manigoat for football. Google search him and look at the film on YouTube.com. I have seen this man score 6-touchdowns in a game in all 3-phases of the Game: Offense, Defense & Special Teams. Now an instructor in the fine art of Football and mentor to many area athletes, he teaches proper techniques so that they can compete on the field and in Life as well.

*Terrence Mann aka "T-Mann"-the former All-American & Mr. Football in Michigan in addition to USA-Today Top-5. In college he was a stand-out for SMU during the Glory Days! Drafted by the Dolphins. He was one of the Top-2 Nose-guards that I ever had to go up against. He was instrumental in my development. After lining up in front of him for 3-years of High School Football & 3-years of Middle School Basketball, his graduation to go to college allowed me to become one of the Best Centers in Detroit & later on one of the Best in the Game!

*Issac "Big-Ike" Readon (NFL/CFL/former NCAA All-American & Div.2 Defensive Player of the Year 85' & Top-3 Rated NG in the draft coming out in 86. Ike is the other Top-NG that I had to go up against and learned a valuable lesson in life. He was a Beast on the Field and a Great Guy off the field. He introduced me to the Real World of College Football and helped me to get my mind right! I passed up going to Clemson because I was trying to avoid running into All-American Nose-guards namely William "The-Refrigerator" Perry & his brother Michael Dean Perry. I signed with a smaller college because I believed that I could go in there and dominate as opposed to sitting on a bench at a major college for 2 years. I was rudely awakened & introduced to the CIAA by Big-Ike as I found out that All-American Football Players came in all shapes, sizes & locations and that if I was ever going to achieve or accomplish anything in Life I had to face challenges head on and not run from them. One of the other lessons that I learned was that the game is 90% mental but on that last 10% you have to put in some work & attack the weights. After 4-semesters in front of Ike, when he graduated & left, so did I. After going up against him, everything else was down hill. I decided that I was made to be "Big-Time & transferred to a Bigger School and unleashed a Beast of my own. I purposed in my Heart that no Nose-Guard would ever get the best of me ever again in Life!

* Jerry Ball (NFL-Detroit Lions/Vikings-This man was a force to be reckoned with. He was like a Pit-bull, not the biggest, but one of the most aggressive non-stop. Not only was he a physical player, but he had the mental game down as well. He would talk you out of your

game if you let him. After a few years of hanging out at the Lions Pre-Season camps during my Collegiate Summer breaks I picked up on various techniques/traits that helped me to elevate my game.

*Darren "Sweet-D" Wilson (USFL-LA-Avengers. He taught me the importance of always looking your best and to always keep your composure under pressure and to never let "them" see you sweat. An important aspect of Life that I learned from him was that if you are late, no amount of rushing or running will make you on time. Travel to arrive alive & sweet-smelling.

*Charles Edward Hugan aka "Big-Hurk"& "Hoagie" (Steelers, Det. Buccaneers and Det. Seminoles: Thanks for teaching me Great techniques during the summer breaks and the significance of O-Line Play + the importance of Beating peoples behind on the line of scrimmage and to do it with a bad attitude. He took me under his wing and showed me how to use my hands and to develop to be a technician of the game. He was one of the founders of the Fraternal Order of Offensive Linemen F.O.O.L for short and we used to do just that, act a fool on the football field. We used to sing & dance and have a good time. Shout out to his brother Byron Culver too! He was a "Blocking Machine!"

*Coach Percy Duhe-RIP- He taught us that *"If you want to be Great, You must do something Extra!"* Also, he emphasized to be careful of the company you keep and not to hang out with bums & drunkards.

*Coach Bill Mars- Thanks for Believing in me and giving me an opportunity.

*Coach Willie Ponton- Taught us that "Whatever *you are lacking in talent you better make up for it with hard work!"*

*Coach Willie Jeffries- One of the first African Americans to become a Head Football Coach at a Division 1 institution who taught us *"Whenever something goes wrong, make sure that you have a Reason and not an Excuse!"*

*Coach Tony Knox-The former All-American Center who became one of my OL coaches towards the end of my College career who was one of the few Centers alive that could stay in front of "Big-Ike" whom he played against in the All American game. He taught me important concepts about life and taking care of your family in addition to advanced techniques of how to shock up through the man in football + important lessons on perseverance.

*Coach Nick Calcutta-One of the Greatest OL coaches in America. This man showed me how to refine my pass-blocking as to where very few got past me after his tutelage. When I took my show on the road, they were amazed!

*The Penn Brothers- Coach William Penn-RIP & Coach Arthur Penn-RIP who owned Penn Sporting Goods and the Northwest Wolverines Youth Football Organization in Detroit, Michigan. They provided opportunities & guidance for many youths {including myself} and their entrepreneurial activities inspired many to continue on to higher education or greater heights.

*Coach Archie "Gunslinger" Cooley- One of the Architects of "The West-Coast" Offense who achieved fame for being the College Coach who made Jerry Rice Nice & also for selling his Offensive package to Bill Walsh of the San Francisco 49'ers who went on to set Records & Win Superbowls with it. Thanks for utilizing our services & for letting me hang around for a season to polish up my game and hone my offensive skills to now dissect Defenses like a frog in a Biology class.

*I want to thank all of the Coaches that were instrumental in my life & development. A lot of the concepts, ideas & philosophies that you helped to instill in me, are still being utilized to this day as well as passed down to generations to come to help produce "Winning Lifestyles".

*I want to thank all of my former teammates. {It was definitely a learning experience. For those of you that got your behinds busted on the field of play {"it's because you didn't attack the weights"}, don't take it personal, it was business. I was just getting you ready for the Real-World and you can probably appreciate me now. What didn't kill you made you stronger? If not, as the Great Coach Casem used to say "They can't take that a_-_ whipping off of them" and you have to respect it! All I wanted to do was "WIN" & if you got in the way, all you became was part of that road that paved the way towards Greatness and becoming a Champion!

*To all of my former & future players: Without you, all of this wouldn't have been possible. Thanks for the Championships and the Championship Rings! Winning is definitely a Lifestyle! (and for those that didn't stay long enough to get a Ring: "A Winner is not a quitter and a Quitter is not a Winner! You'll WIN if you don't Quit & get your mind Right!" It's Real on the Field! It's not "Play-station or X-Box." Most Important: "Keep Your Head on a Swivel on the field & in life because someone is always looking to take it off!" **Stop the Excuses** & put your mind to good use. *"A mind is a terrible thing to waste."* Get in front of a mirror and repeat after me: **"Everyday I go to sleep as a Winner & wake up as a CHAMPION!"** If any of you ever need me, don't hesitate to reach out & contact me or call, because "Teamwork makes the Dream Work" & "Success in Life is a Team Effort!"

*Mr. Russell Chew- Owner of Chew's Beauty Supply & Manufacturing who showed me the importance of flowing in the *"Spirit"* when making decisions in addition to showing me another level of the Business side of the *"Hair-Game"*. As an intern with them during my college years I learned the importance of Distribution channels & connectivity.

"You can have the best product in America, but if no one knows that you exist or if you can't get the product to the people it will go undersold!"

Check out his annual International Hair Show www.ChewsHairAffair.com & get up his new signature air fragrance.

The Detroit Buccaneers, The Dallas Cowboys, The Detroit Lions, Shawn Johnson, Charles Wiley with Infinity Web Design, C.E. Wiley Studios & 504-Dymes-B.R., La. Coach Mike Tyson, Anthony Brooks(Scoops Barbershop, *Kirk Anthony Jackson III aka "Big-Tre"-RIP, Coach Vanzant, Coach McClung, Kim Brown, Coach Robert Bishop, Danielle Fluker aka "The Princess", Carla McClatty,

*Coach & Trainer Sharee Thompson- Former SEC & European Basketball star, now one of the Top female Basketball & Fitness trainers in the DFW-Metroplex & Orlando who is serious about her craft. In the true sense of the word "Champion", she finds a way to Win. www.tSportsFit.com

*Coach Terrell Woody- He is a Trainer of some of the NBA's elite players & Draft prospects. He is also a Facilitator of the "Swisher-Courts" Sports Complex/ Athletic facility in Lewisville, Texas where they transform projects into legitimate prospects.

*Hampton University- This is A Beautiful Place. It is 3/5th surrounded by water & had me feeling like I was on "**Fantasy Island**". The Va. Beach was stupendous. I definitely got a chance to experience how the Rich live and didn't want to give up that lifestyle. They were true to their image with all of the Beautiful & Intelligent people on campus. www.HamptonU.edu

*Howard University, They let you know Day-1 that you were "**Cream of the Crop**" & "**The Best of the Best**" and what a privilege it was to be enrolled here, for every person enrolled, 10k had tried & applied! We were taught that it wasn't anything that we couldn't achieve or receive if we put our minds to it! The main thing that I liked about this school was that creativity was encouraged and **they didn't teach or train you to be a slave, graduate and always work for someone else, but more so to eventually take ownership of your situation** and not to despise small beginnings. **Academics came first** and **sports were actually an extracurricular activity** and not a job. **They placed a "Priority" on Intelligence and the classroom setting was "Highly Competitive"** to say the least. **Some of the most intelligent & elite individuals in the country have matriculated at this institution** of higher learning. www.Howard.edu

*Southern University & A&M College- This is a place that **"Reigns Supreme in Sports"** & has **"One of The BEST Bands in The Land"** due to the massive amounts of time, energy and effort put into practice & preparation for these events. **"They are Serious about the Product that they**

display or put upon The Field or Court of Play!" At Southern, If you can't *"cut the mustard", they will CUT YOU & Your $ Too! As one famous former Coach used to say "Cut-Away Holmes" or "You Better Get You Some Stay Here!" At first it was a culture shock*, but we learned how to adapt & adjust to overcome the obstacles of life in addition to dealing with the masses of the people. The cream will definitely rise to the Top! **It was a true learning experience to get you ready for the real world.** We learned to develop networking skills early on. It was evident that it wasn't always what or who you know, but more so to whom you are connected to and who knows you. www.SUBR.edu

*LSU- Some of the Greatest Athletes that ever played the game wore Purple & Gold! This was one place where fan participation definitely played a role in the outcomes of some games! They don't call it "Death Valley" for nothing! Whenever the football team scored you could hear the roar & feel the vibrations like an earthquake miles away! www.LSU.edu

*Cooley High School-Detroit, Mi. **Home of The Champions!** *"Where the Strong Survive & the rest get eaten alive!"* This is where I learned the art of the *"Killer-Instinct"* mindset in athletics, academics & sometimes on my daily journey to school because Champions Always Find a Way to Win! We were taught to Win with class and have good sportsmanship but to also *"kill a knat with a sledge-hammer & to cut the rope when your opponent is hanging off of the cliff!"* The 5 or 6 teams that could say they won against us in a 4-year period never wanted to line up against or play us again nor were they ever the same after playing against us. Most of them took 2-3 weeks to recuperate or rehab from injuries after playing us. The training that I received here was similar to that of "Special-Forces" training which turned some of us into 1-man army's /wrecking crews. One on one, we were never to get beat by 1 man. The motto of the day was *"if you can't win, don't lose"* and I still operate by some of those same philosophies today.

*Professor Katrice Albert & Professor Barbara Thomas at Southern Univ.-BR. These 2-ladies helped me to develop into the Marketing Genius that I am today. After winning the *"Mr. Marketing"* award in 91' in the School of Business the sky was the limit after that! We also helped to develop "*T.T. Allain` Day" where everybody came to school freshly dressed {due to the Recruiters we were attracting from major corporations} now known as "Pretty Wednesday" on campus which was also the inspiration for the hit song.*

*Professor Earl Marcelle at Southern Univ.-BR. He taught us the important concept of "*C.Y.A*" (*Cover Your Assets* along with how to prepare and avoid the "*Games & Tricks*" that people play in Corporate America. The Valuable Lessons that he taught us were instrumental in my development.

*Agent & Atty. Tim Crawford (All I can say is ***"Thoroughly Impressive" & THANK YOU!***

*Thomas "Hitman" Hearns aka "The Motor City Cobra"(**6-time World Champion Boxer** who taught me that *if you believe in yourself and what you are doing to* *invest time into yourself to be the best that you can be so that when opportunity presents itself you can be in a position to receive.*

*Shout-out to my future wife.

*Noel Scarlet- Former NFL Player- Cowboys/Vikings who now Coaches, trains & prepares prospects for the combine & the next level. When the game is on the line, who do you want to find? Check out www.4th-and-inches.com

*George Teague & Family- First you mystified us when picked off that interception and ran it back to win the National Championship at Alabama and then again on Thanksgiving day to knock my Lions out of the playoffs when you were with Green Bay. Then you brought tears to my eyes when you *knocked Terrell Owens off of the star at Cowboys Stadium.* You never ceased to amaze me. www.GeorgeTeagueandFriends.com

*Francious Faulkner- One of the top "Print-Designers & Embroiders of the Future", that's been putting it down for decades consistently

since my college days. If you ever need a large amount of work done right the first time in a short amount of time look him up www.IceWorldInc.biz

*Rocky Parker (Rocky came up with a nice concept for student athletes to show them proper form, competitiveness & sportsmanship. Check out www.TexasSchoolOfFootball.com

*Clay Mack (D1-Sports Sports Complex-Dallas, TX. He is one of the top Trainers and Secondary Coaches in the Metroplex. If he can't get your footwork right, then you're in the wrong occupation.

*Coach Chris Givens-Thanks for helping me when I needed it the most! My career might have been over before it started if it wasn't for you! Thanks for the expert tutelage.

*Mechelle Williams-Ambit Energy Company; Not only can she help you to save Considerably on your Electricity Bills {Residential & Commercial} but can help you to make $ as well. Check out www.mewill.Energy526.com And start saving Today.

*Norman Sparrow-owner of restaurant "The Table is Bread" in B.R., La. www.TableIsBread.net

*Tarsha Polk (www.TheMarketingLady.com) This lady can give you insight on bringing your business to light!

*Deborah Dillard {the President of Social Media Voice-Dialogue Management Solutions. Whenever you need to give your product or service a voice on Social Media, hit her up. www.SocialMediaVoice.net

*Coach John Montgomery {Thanks for giving me a fair-chance and an opportunity to showcase my skills. It was hard, but it was fair! One of your greatest attributes was your ability to communicate with your players and get them to visualize the task at hand. Also, that left-handed stance that you taught for OT's came in handy on the next level. I appreciate the experience.

*Coach Ralph Williams- Thanks for your expert tutelage & assistance: Most of all, thanks for coming to pick me up the morning of the Nichols St. game, I will be forever grateful & telling my Grandkids or somebody

else's grandkids about you. If they had more football coaches like you that actually cared about their players as a person, instead of just what can you do for me on the field/ or what have you done for me lately, this would be a better sport, but in my own words," It's not a nice game!"

*Randy Manning-a former team-mate who put me up on extra "*game*" to go with the terrain when I transferred down south. He showed me how to apply my entrepreneurial skills and to network to greater heights. He stressed the importance of looking good, playing good & getting good grades to break the stereotype of the typical athlete. We weren't just 2 of the best dressed "*Big-Men*" on campus; we were 2-of the Best Dressed on campus period from head to toe.

We didn't go to the show, we were the Show & when we showed up, and we Showed Out! On the field & off! He also showed me how to apply the accounting concepts of "*Assets & Liabilities*" and" *Debits & Credits*" to real life scenarios and to take inventory of those on my personal team. Randy stressed the importance of staying focused & to *"make the money and not chase the honeys"*.

*Coach Pete Richardson (You took winning to another level! They need to name a stadium after you!

*Coach Bill Williamson and Coach Willard Bailey- Anytime you are ready to start another program, hit me up! I am the man with the plan!

*Coach Jack Phillips {A former NFL Player - Chiefs/ College Coach & former teammate of mine that has a passion for the game. Best known for his relentless play as a player & a technician of the game, Jack is now getting the best out of his players as a Coach and a Trainer. He is highly regarded as a *"Master of Secondary Play"*.

*Dr. Penny St. James- Entrepreneurial Business Centers of America / The St. James Marketing Agency.

*Marlon Edwards (He got our vote for "Small Business Entrepreneur of The Year" with "Suave-Handyman-Mechanic & Moving Services"-Dallas, TX. Where they bring the repairs to you! Everybody needs a Handyman!

*Dr. Krystal Barnett-Frisco, TX.- This is **one of the finest Doctors in America & she doesn't use scalpels nor needles!** At her office they get your body tight & right plus keep your health and nutrition on point naturally without drugs or pharmaceuticals. Definitely the wave of the future! Check out www.DrKrystalBarnett.com ; www.DrKrystalExtraordinaryHealth.com and www.MaximizedLiving.com you will be glad you did!

*Joe Bean {Commissioner of the SAFL-Football League, NAACP-Regional Representative and producer of the La. HS-Senior Bowl. A former teammate who always stood for what he believed in and gave 100% on the field and never quit in the face of adversity. Thanks for the hook-up! www.logoserver.com/SAFL.html

*Dr. Tray Andrews -DC. - Owner of the Lake Houston Wellness Center near Houston, TX. This is another one of the finest Doctors in America & she doesn't use scalpels nor needles either! *She is serious about her*

trade & her craft. www.LakeHoustonWellness.com

*Ozell Graham at The Fade Shop-Dallas, TX www.FadeShop.com {**winners of The Chosen One Sports: "*People's Choice*" Award**. The owner-Ozell took a concept that he developed in the military and turned it into a Franchise in the civilian world. You can get your top cropped & your shoes shined at the same time! If you're ever in Dallas, TX stop through. You may be surprised as to who you may run into up in there.

*Travis Pearson- Barber in Dallas, TX. Who not only is sharp at his craft, but has the business side of the game down so good that he spends about as much time on the golf course as he does in the shop.

*Crystal- owner of Eye Candy-Waxing & Threading Brow Salon -Dallas, TX www.EyeCandyBrowSalon.com

*Tye Diggs {He is known as "The King of Parties" Host, Singer, Song-writer & Promoter-Dallas, TX.

*Mike Chatman- Once a "Cold-Blooded" Kick-Returner & RB, now owner of Chatman Realty & Reliable Tax Returns-Dallas/Ft. Worth, TX . "Changing Real-Estate 1-Smile at a Time!" www.MichaelDChatman.Kw.realty.com and www.ReliableTaxReturnsSrv.com

*Terrance *"Abdullah"* Sanders aka "Coach-Tiny" (NFL-Giants/Browns & now owner of Powerhouse Pro-Style Training-Arlington, TX. A former teammate that went to almost as many colleges as I did. Now training Champions. Legendary Hall of Fame Coach Bill Parcels gave him the name "Tiny" and it stuck with him. www.ProStyleTraining.net

*John Breen-Photography-Dallas, TX. One of the Best in Town & One of the Best Around! www.BreenPhotography.com

*BJ. Jackson {The owner of Prema Day Spa Plano, TX. "Royal Treatment at Reasonable Rates" www.PremaDaySpa.net

*Kateria Baggett aka "Lady-T"- One of the hottest up & coming female radio personalities in the DFW-Metroplex! Check her out www.LadyTsaySomething.com

*Bishop Dwight Pate - founder of Church Point Ministries & WNDC-AM Radio-B.R, La. This man always has an encouraging word that's uplifting. Check out his book "I Think I Thought I Knew!!!" www.BishopDwightPate.com

*Coach Petaway-Detroit Buccaneers. This was a man of principles. I apologize for getting thrown out of the Semi-final game & costing our team the chance to play in the championship. The guy had hit me with a "cheap-shot" & I retaliated. It was a lesson in Life. Since then I have learned how to control my "Inner-Ike" to play & (now coach) within the confines of the rules of the game. I further developed my concepts of good sportsmanship to realize that sometimes one's actions affect more than oneself and that you have to operate for the common good of the team even if it means waiting for the next play or *"taking one for the team!"*

*Coach Cunningham-Detroit Buccaneers. He emphasized certain principles of manhood including the fact that a man must have a job & that a job is what's necessary! His words of wisdom helped me to stay focused and put things in proper perspective including a better outlook on life; because I was about to quit a "high-dollar" paying job that I liked to play the game that I loved.

*Coach Kelley Goodman –The former NFL-Player & Coach who helped me to develop & master my *"board-skills"* to an unbelievable level through competition and brain-storming sessions. Also, I had to borrow a couple of those good theories & techniques to pass along to my players and put in my *"pamphlet."*

*Devin Wyman-Author, Coach, Evangelist & Former NFL/AFL Great with the Patriots, Vikings & San Jose Saber-cats, Now doing a Great Work for The Lord and in the Community. *"Hard work pays off!"* www.TheWinningEdge.US

*Terry Glenn-Former All-American Player@ Ohio St. & NFL Star with the Patriots & Cowboys/Offensive Coordinator for the Texas Revolution–Indoor Football/Arena Championship Team 2015'. His approach to the game sets him apart from the Rest.

*Donald Campbell-*aka Bishop Don "Magic" Juan* - Author & Consultant to the stars. Stresses the importance of being true to the game & that whatever you do, *"Take GOD with You"*!

*Shay Ashford-The Ultimate Reality Shows-she came in and saw the vision and embraced it. Thank You for utilizing and encompassing a lot of my clients in your endeavors.

*Reynaldo Rey-RIP {Comedian & mentor to one of my good friends.

*Torrence Williams- Photographer-Dallas, TX. Has one to the Top-Modeling Portfolios in the State!

*Allison C. Tucker Jr. Best known as "The Silent Partner" is One of the Top concert & event promoters in TEXAS. Working smoothly behind the scenes, he makes things happen on a Large Scale. www.TheSilentPartner.biz

*Dr. Hank Seitz - World renowned author & Business Coach who helps positively motivated sales professionals create more clients, cash and time using a proven success

formula. Check out his books "Think, Feel and Grow Rich" & "The Happiest Man In the World" and Enrich Yourself. If you need to *"fuel-inject"* your business, hit him up and tell him that we sent you! www.ThinkFeelAndGrowRich.US ; www.DrHankSeitz.com

*Big Daddie the DJ - One of New Orleans finest & a popular Radio DJ in the Dallas/ Ft. Worth area. If he can't get your event cranking, you don't have one. www.bdTHEDJ.com

*BIG-D AUTOMOTIVE-Dallas, Texas. Thanks for keeping my foreign whips on "Tight Grips" & maintaining them at the "Players-Price" because *Important* things are riding on my tires and Proper Maintenance is Essential!

*Ellen Ellis- Fashion Designer & Owner of A.O.S. Sportswear & Swimwear.

*Coach Alonzo Carter-A Coach who is making a difference in the lives of young men as well as on the field in Junior College Football and now Major College Football as well.

*Chef Joseph Randall II - The CEO of Nana's Barbecue & catering in Allen, TX. Where they

bring /or ship the "Q" to You www.NanasBBQ.com First impressions are lasting impressions and I was impressed! Falls off the bone & mouth watering!

*Tudi Wilson- aka *'Tudilicious"* who achieved fame on the FOX Reality show "Master Chef "-Season 2 and for her Gourmet BBQ Sauces. www.tudilicious.com

*Chef Keith Hicks & the owners Herb & Caroline of Button's Restaurant in Ft. Worth, TX. www.ButtonsRestaurant.com This is one of my favorite places in Dallas to go relax & unwind after a long week. The atmospheres & the cuisine are unmatched. Chef Keith Hick's signature dishes & The Live Bands performing simultaneously make for an unbeatable combination. Also a Great Place to Network & the Sunday Brunches are memorable.

*Corey Austin- an impact player and owner of a Waffle House franchise in Rockwall, TX. Thanks for making a difference & sponsoring the All-star Game & my youth organization. We gave the phrase "Time to Eat" a whole new meaning.

*Special Shout-Out to Lewis H. Williams III with the "I Hustle Nation" down in Houston, TX. www.iHustleNation.com (One of the "Ultimate Hustlers" who has revolutionized the game & mapped out blueprints for success and how to win in life with his books, videos, radio-blogs & events.

*Monte Tayion Holland-A former teammate of my brother's that went from Corporate Executive to a Corporate Tycoon as owner of Tayion clothing company which is in my opinion one of the smoothest & flavorful custom clothing lines around that's "so fresh & so clean". See for yourself www.Tayion.com . If you don't know, now you Know! "They put the "ooth" in Smooth & have "Big-Fella" sizes too!

*David Mott-This guy has been "Good-People" & down since day-1. I observed how he transformed a corporate 401k into a Corporation & a tourist attraction in the "Greek-town" section of downtown Detroit, Mi. that's been in business over a decade and ships-Worldwide.
www.GoodPeoplePopcorn.com "Where the People & the Popcorn make the Difference."

*Connie Morgan-CEO-AMPS Magazine-Dallas, Texas. Whenever you need the "Amp" turned up on your business, product, service or project, consult with them www.dallas.amspmagazine.com

*Teddy Davey -The Owner of The Balcony Club {#1 Jazz Bar in Dallas. Whenever you need to relax your mind so you can concentrate or interview a prospective new client or a date, this is the place to relax & unwind. The music is pure & refreshing and the atmosphere is laid back. A lot of the top Jazz artists have passed through here. www.TheBalconyClub.com

*Coach John Carroll - President & Head Coach of the North Texas Cowboys Youth Football organization. www.ntxcowboys.org

*DeAndre Jackson- Former CFL & AFL football player now turned businessman and Owner of "**Winners BBQ**" in Plano, Texas who is "*Smoking the Competition!*" With a product that separates them from the rest, they are a *Candidate* for the Chosen One Sports-"People's Choice" Award for one of the Top Barbeque spots in town. See for yourself www.WinnersBBQ.com

*Lincoln Parks aka *"LP"* & *"Billionaire Bruce Wayne"*-The underground rapper, actor; Radio show host, model & musician who hails from Flint, Michigan transformed his career using major mainstream moves. Tired of the games people played in the entertainment industry, he went solo and kicked it off with his first album *"Black Sunday"* which was a classic and came back a few years later with the *"Bruce Wayne"* album which confirmed the status of who he is. His LIVE shows are something to see! Check him out on www.BillionaireBruceWayne.weebly.com

*Sharon Poole-The Dallas Morning News. She was referred to us for our outstanding services and she made an instant impact by inviting me to tap into her networks and associations to achieve optimal results after viewing my manuscripts. She is definitely an asset to their publication as well as the community.

*Kia Davis aka *"Kia-D"*-The Dynamic Show Host & Radio Personality for www.WeTalkRadio.com

*Kevin Poole Jr.- The Owner of "WE EDIT SPORTS USA" who came in the second half of

the game on these books and literally put points on the board in a short amount of time. Their commercials, video graphics & logo spins are *"Amazingly Unique"* which helped my products to *"OUTSTANDING"* in a highly competitive market. They offer a myriad of services including equipment rental for making *"High-Quality"* films in addition to creating Highlight films that will get you noticed in the sports realm. Check out www.WeEditSportsUSA.com

*Kisha Taylor-The owner of "American Soul Café' & Catering" + "The Grill Café" –Dallas, TX where they put their *"Heart & Soul"* into Every Meal & they deliver and *"Bring the Soul to You!"* Event Planning is also a Specialty. *www.AmericanSoulCafe.com* & *www.TheGrillHouseCafe.com*

*Mathew Whittier -The Vice President & Co-owner of Offense-Defense camps which provides enrichment opportunities for Football Players and Coaches nationwide. www.O-D.com

*Marvin-Owner of "MARVELOUS LIMOUSINES' -Detroit, MI. where they give a Limousine Ride a Whole New Feel.

*Connie Arceneaux - Owner of Phenomenal Palace Salon-Houston, TX, and also happens to own a Promotions company complete with "Street Teams." If you're ever in the Houston market or trying to get in, hit her up to get your event, product or service to "Blow-up!"

*Dr. Jen Welter aka "Coach Jen" {She is formerly one of the top female athletes in the world & the first to play & Coach professional football with men, now working as a sports psychologist and trainer to the stars. If you need motivation, inspiration or encouragement or if your mind or your game needs strengthening, look her up: www.JenWelter.com *"If you want to Win, put Coach Jen In!"*

*Brian Pearson -Service Manager at the Brakes Plus in Frisco, Texas. All I can say is that when you drive a Benz or any other high-end vehicle and you're trying to win or make ends, you need a friend on your team that specializes in keeping you rolling at the player's price or team rate! Proper maintenance is essential, and when they go down, you still need to get around. Just like in the "Pros" *you can't make the club in the* *tub"*, **it's hard to make a cent if you're not at the event!** www.brakesplus.com

*Kyle Whitley with Whitley Ink & Whitley Inc.

*Bro. Gilbert Melendez, www.DallasTicketsUSA.com owner of one of the top Ticket Brokerages in the Dallas/ Ft. Worth area who gives back to the community with his weekly Bible-studies and feeding of the homeless & hungry both spiritually & literally. If you ever need tickets to any major sporting event or entertainment activity, spend your money where you know your seed is going to be multiplied and uplift the community at the same time.

*Tommy Benizio - Former Commissioner of the IFL & CEO of the Texas Revolution-Arena Football team. www.TexasRevs.com I want to thank you for allowing me to come in and apply some of the principles in my books to help motivate & inspire the team to overcome adversity, deaths and injuries to achieve greatness by reaching the Championship.

*Bruce Badgett- Owner of Champions Edge Energy Sports Drink

www.GetChampionsEdge.com & part owner of The Dallas Sidekicks –Professional Indoor Soccer Team www.DallasSidekicks.com . While we were on the road to success & the Championship, we were sipping on *"Bruce-Juice"* aka-*"Champions Edge Energy Sports Drink"*.

*DeForest Hart- Director of America's Next Draft Pick Reality Show. www.AmericasNextDraftPick.com

*Darius Fudge-All-star Arena Football Player & Accountant with SMD Consulting & Accounting who not only put up good numbers on the field, but can help you to accumulate good numbers on your financial statement and in your bank account! www.SMDaccounting.com

*Carlandre Bussey- Former Champion Football Player now manager of *"The Inspiration Band"* which when they perform, it's not just a show, but an *Experience!* www.InspirationBand.com

*Candace "Mahogany" Miller aka "Mahogany the Artist" (Musician/ Instructor, Band Director; Contemporary Jazz Artist & Praise

Team Leader who is multi-faceted versatile and extremely talented. She not only shares the knowledge of her gifts through a program and Music School that she developed called *"Jazz BeCuzz"*, she practices what she preach and gives back as a Praise Team Leader at a Major Church in North Dallas. Experience the many facets of her endeavors: www.jazzbecuzzac.com ; www.mahoganytheartist.com ; https://candacemahoganymiller.bandcamp.com/releases

*Tim Brown-The Heisman Trophy Winner from Notre Dame & NFL-HOF Great from the Oakland Raiders. Now GM/owner of the Texas Revolution-Arena Football team.

*Jameis Winston-The Heisman Trophy Winner/National Champion from Florida State who was also first round draft pick of the Tampa Bay Buccaneers.

*Vincent "V.C." Castile -aka *"The Celebrity Barber"* in Dallas, Texas. Making the World Famous one cut at a time, he is best known in the Hair-Game for innovative promotions & for having more Celebrities & Professional Athletes as clients than the next 2-

contenders combined. Check out his website www.CelebrityBarber.com & get a clue as to what's really going on.

*Jeff Davis {More than just a "*World Class Barber*" but an upper echelon experience. The concept and atmosphere that he provides not only allows you to relax your mind so that you can concentrate, but treat yourself to an "in-town" get away. Look up www.WorldClassBarber.com and www.AstuteGentlemen.com {I was Impressed.

*Lawrence Mann- "A Man of many talents!" Owner of the Top Achievers Training Program and the Director of the Mann Up Program for Plano, Schools. He is known as one of the Top Basketball Recruiters and AAU-Coaches in North Texas. One of his specialties is Photography & Graphic Art which brings photos to life. Check out www.TopAchieversPlano.org & www.LawrenceMannPhotography.com

*Aerosmith {shout-out to all the guys in the band who supported us in our efforts. www.AerosmithTribute.com

*Earl Lloyd-RIP -The father of one of my good friends Kevin and the First African-American Player & Coach in the NBA. He paved the way and helped to create many opportunities for others through his hard work and perseverance. His legacy lives on & will soon have a postal stamp with his image. Pick up his book: "Moon Fixer" available on www.Amazon.com and in major bookstores. Also make sure that you go check out the movie detailing his life entitled "THE FIRST TO DO IT!" www.TheFirstToDoIt.com

*Arthur Muhammad - Owner/Film Director & Producer of the movie "CARTER HIGH". We are thankful that he has allowed us to participate in the movie and to help promote it Nationwide to bring insight to players on all levels. He overcame insurmountable odds to fund & film this movie which will be a staple in every football lover's movie catalog & collection. This is a Prime Example of how "You can Win if You Don't Quit!" Check it out www.TheCarterHighMovie.com and his other works www.SweetChariotFilms.com ; https://pro-labs.imdb.com/name/nm2584377

Dr. George C. Fraser -This man was a guest on one of our Radio shows and blew our mind in a short period of time. He runs the "Power Networking Conference" and opened our eyes to some alarming facts to make us more aware of our surroundings and those we surround ourselves with. "If your 5-Closest Friends aren't worth at least $500,000 collectively, then you have a lot of work to do!" "67% of most people that graduate from college never open or read another book in their life." He not only laced us up with information on how to Successfully multiply your seeds to achieve generational wealth and empower your offspring for the next two generations to come, but plugged us into his concept of "Learn, Earn & Return". For more knowledge that they don't teach in College, check out www.FraserNet.com

*Jerry Jones (owner of the Dallas Cowboys-NFL www.DallasCowboys.com Check out his book **"PLAYING TO WIN."***

**The other Big-Ray (Entrepreneur/ part owner of the Allen Arena Football team & Big-Ray's BBQ-Allen, TX. (

www.BigRaysBarbeque.com if you're ever in town, come around and ask for the "Big Ray $pecial!" *"We have that flavor that you savor & a price that's nice!"*

*Special Note:

 With $uccess in Life being a Team-Effort, you are going to need as many avenues as you can get to promote your product, service, theme or cause in the guise of Branding/Marketing and Name Recognition. It's a numbers game. In order to achieve your goal, you will need a certain number/quantity and quality of people to subscribe to your theory, products or services. Feel free to utilize or contact some of the aforementioned resources if you have a "Need" that needs to be supplied within their area of expertise and ***don't forget to ask for "The Big-Ray $pecial!"*** *You may be surprised as to what the power of divine connections can do for you and yours.*

*We give **Thanks and Glory to GOD** for allowing us to have this network, associations & divine connections. We would also like to thank all of the Scouts, Recruiters, Players, Coaches, Camp-Directors and CHAMPIONS that came through Chosen One Sports (www.Chosen1Sports.com) & the Supports Staff   for   all   of   their   assistance   and patronage. *"Many were called, few were Chosen..."* **CHAMPIONS ALWAYS FIND A WAY TO WIN!**   With you we achieved Extraordinary RESULTS! "Greatness is not a Coincidence!" Together-Everybody-Achieves-More! If you ever have a Sports Related product, movie, event or concept that you need marketed, promoted or introduced into diverse target markets or need Sports figures/ actors to appear in movie premiers, *hit them up at* (972)CHOSEN-1

**Last but not the least, we would like to thank   everybody   on   the   TEAM   at www.BigRayInternational.com   where "Winning is a Lifestyle"-Embrace It! Their hard work and dedication paid off.

If **You Need Connections, Contacts & Information** to have a Book, Event, Radio Talk-show, product, service or (concept that you   developed)   marketed,   promoted   & introduced into diverse target markets.   Hit them up online, email: PromoteYourself@BigRayInternational.com or CALL on the *"Big-Ray International"* hotline.

"We can have your phone Blowing up like a Volcano!"

"Sometimes it's not the amount of times that you try, but more-so the means by which one is willing to go through to achieve their objective!"

The Bottom Line: **"WE GET RESULTS!"**

www.MillionDollarSideHustle.com

www.Chosen1Sports.com

www.BigRayInternational.com

www.48LawsOfWinning.com

www.WinningIsALifestyle.com